Survival

Preparedness

Tips

Volume I

Sam Spencer

www.survivalpreparednesstips.com

info@survivalpreparednesstips.com

ISBN 13: 978-1-938091-50-6

DEDICATION

This book is dedicated to those individuals who are not sure how to prepare for disaster, to those are looking for real answers, and to those who need just a little help to fine tune their disaster planning

About The Author

Sam Spencer has been actively involved in personal preparedness for over 40 years. He has studied many disasters over the years, both natural and man-caused. Throughout his research he has developed and improved numerous ideas for survival preparedness. Sam's streamlined and simplified disaster and survival techniques are organized for reliable results.

As an author, he has written several volumes to help the prudent minded. His book *Food Storage Made Easy, A Practical Approach*, simplifies food storage principles. Sam's personal practices of a lifetime enrich his practical approach. Referencing one's chosen diet, the reader finds the book provides practical answers to personal food storage questions.

Sam has authored and produced a book accompanied by two DVD's titled, *Drying Fruits And Vegetables Made Easy*. The work teaches in a simple and illustrated manner what Sam has practiced for many years. He informs in easy-to-follow terms the oldest method of preserving foods. Those who have followed his instructions have added healthy foods without preservatives or additives to their personal diets and food storage.

Year after year he produces a backyard garden that provides a year's worth of food for him and his wife. From practical backyard gardening techniques he has developed with a lifetime of preparedness thinking. Much of his garden produce is shared with others as he encourages them to develop their own personal preparedness program. He encourages others to garden even a little to learn now and be ahead of the learning curve if the need to live on your garden arises.

Over the years he has taught various preparedness classes and tutored many individuals as they developed practical, personal preparedness programs. These many lessons, taught and the sharing of much practical advice, have led to his writings. Now, in book form, Sam is sharing his experiences and ideas with all who wish to become better prepared.

Sam will tell you that "Preparation eliminates fear. It will give you confidence in crisis. You don't have to spend much money to be prepared!" Many people seek him out for his knowledge, guidance and ideas.

Sam and his wife Patrice live in Utah and are the parents of six children and the grandparents of eight. Sam Spencer is certainly someone that you would want on your team.

CONTENTS

Introduction

Over the years I have studied many disasters and asked myself, "What do I need to do to prepare myself for such an occurrence?" I have seen the unfortunate victims' glaring deficiencies in each disaster. In many cases shortcomings were exceptionally evident. From these observations I continually tweak my emergency preparedness items to be able to satisfy the different scenarios that might happen. The only way to truly understand these sequence of events is to study each disaster. The people's needs must be specified in order to implement a solution that works for them. Finally a person must decide which scenarios fit their needs and take appropriate actions.

For example, in Hurricane Katrina it seemed like the people and the government were so ill prepared with even the basics such as water. It seems so simple and so basic yet water was probably the biggest single survival issue that I noticed from what I reviewed. In addition, the government's planning was shortsighted. The community as a whole expected the government to save them.

In the year 2008 there was an earthquake on February 21 in Wells, Nevada. There was snow on the ground and it was cold. There were no services for a week. No natural gas for heat. No electricity to run the heaters and the lights. Plus there was no water and consequently the toilets would not work.

As I studied this earthquake, which was basically in my backyard, I imagined that this could very easily have happened to me as I live in the Salt Lake Valley with the Wasatch fault right below me. I paid

particular attention to the hardships that the Wells, Nevada citizens had to endure. What would I do without power? How would I heat my home if we had no natural gas? Did I have enough water? As I pondered these questions I reviewed my own disaster preparedness planning.

What were the things I needed to do to make sure I was not caught so unprepared like my neighbors in Wells, Nevada?

Since I already have my house set up with emergency power I checked and ran my generator to make sure that my power backup system was in excellent operating condition. I then began to examine my preparedness plan for an alternate heat source. I inventoried and increased my water storage. The Wells, Nevada quake came during the coldest days of the winter with temperatures below freezing even throughout the day.

After several weeks of analyzing the quake, pondering and planning solutions, I made additional major changes in my preparedness plan. It is very important that with each disaster, no matter where it is in the world that you analyze the event. Pay specific attention to the needs of the individuals, particularly those needs that are hard to meet. Picture your family as the people in crisis and see yourself acting in each situation. Armed with new information, improve your plan to become better prepared. You will be able to save yourself!

From the earthquakes in Chile, I observed that many of the buildings did not totally collapse. Some slid off their foundations and stayed together. Some suffered minor damage but were indeed damaged. However, what stuck out the most was that many of the structures were parallelograms, slightly leaning but had not totally collapsed. They were still uninhabitable, looking like a wooden box that had fallen off the back of a truck.

The building codes in Utah, where I live, like Chile, are very strict when it comes to earthquake guidelines. With so many internal walls, sheer walls and metal strapping, we will probably experience similar results. I now have stored at my house some 4" x 4" 10' posts that could be used to support my structure, or to sure up the structure from further damage. It also became obvious to me that if I had a partial collapse, it might be difficult for me to get to my preparedness items. After some review I've also made changes to ensure better access to my preparedness supplies.

From the recent hurricane Sandy, as with other disasters, a few things stood out. One I particular was that people were expecting the government to help. My question is: is help coming from the government an oxymoron? This is why your personal preparedness is so important and you cannot count on the federal, state or local governments to save you. My recommendation is that you prepare so you can save yourself.

The unprepared people in hurricane Sandy could have made life more comfortable if only they had prepared in reserve just one week's worth of food and water! That simple preparedness step could have helped many. Many were caught off guard with either no working appliances or no back-up emergency cooking facilities. If they had implemented one of the emergency cooking tips from this book it would have made a great difference for them. There are excellent and inexpensive ideas in this book to do just that! Simply preparing today will save a lot of trouble later!

I will share with you in this book several ideas that would have saved the disaster victims, and even possibly you, int the future, an awful lot of discomfort. However, the information in this book will do you no good unless you make a plan that is designed for you, by you, and then implemented by you. So begin to plan even if your plan allows only for a few weeks of survival. Your emergency program should be sacred to you. Maintain it current so that when you need it everything will be in order.

With all due respect do not count on FEMA or any other government agency to satisfy your needs. If by chance they do help then be sure to tell them "thank you." My father used to always say, "If you want the job done right, do it yourself." That is particularly good advice, especially when it comes to emergency preparedness and survival planning.

As you read this book you will find numerous ideas that interest you. There are plenty more to come. Study them! Analyze your situation and finally put in place a plan designed by you--- for you. You will find a "shopping list" at the end of each list to make it easy to implement.

A little knowledge and a few precautionary measures can enormously increase your chances of surviving any disaster. The keys are education, planning and preparation. The safety tips that follow will not make you an expert. Knowing these tips will save property and lives in a disaster situation. Invest in this knowledge and preparation so that you can "weather the storm" in a magnificent manner.

You will notice that with every disaster discussed in this book there are three basic steps to survival preparedness. Learn the steps and apply them to the types of disasters that are most common to your area. Imagine you and your family experiencing the disaster and envision your successful survival of each event because you have planned in advance and have executed your plan well.

Three Step Plan:

1. **Get Educated**. Learn what to do before during and after a disaster.
2. **Make a plan**. Design a plan for you and your family keeping in mind individual needs and locations.
3. **Prepare survival kits.** This should include at least a 72 hour kit for each person in your household. It should also include long term survival preparedness items based on your plan.

Get prepared today!

Survival

Preparedness

Tips

Water Storage Tips

Water of course is absolutely necessary for survival. A person can survive easily for one week without food. I have often heard stories of people surviving for several weeks without food. However, without water they will die within a few days. It is for this reason that you must store emergency water. We are accustomed to abundant domestic water supplies and we can hardly imagine water not being available. We take it for granted.

An interruption in water supply does not necessarily come from a natural disaster. It can also come from other sources such as: a contaminated water supply; a broken water main; or even failed equipment at the utility. A good idea to have a minimum of one week's worth of water stored for all occupants of your home or apartment. You will see how simple this can be as you study this section.

One gallon per person per day is the minimum that you should have in storage. This will give you two quarts to drink each day and two quarts for cooking and brushing your teeth. If you would like more water for hygiene, then you will need one additional gallon per person per day. The ideal amount of water to store for an emergency is two gallons per person per day. That would mean 14 gallons of emergency water per person per week. I have stored in my garage a few 55 gallon drums of water. I consider that one drum is two gallons a day for one person for 30 days. That seems like a lot but it all depends on your method and location of storing the water.

Hot weather can increase the amount of water needed. Children may need additional water. People who are ill, pregnant, and nursing will also need additional drinking water. Limiting your activity particularly in hot weather can decrease your demand for water. It is important however, that you give your body the water that it needs each day. **Stay hydrated!**

When disaster strikes, your emergency water storage could save your life. Have enough emergency water! Minimum 7 days worth of water per person!

How Much Water Should You Store?

The answer to this question is very simple: store one gallon of water per person per day of anticipated emergency. Generally it takes a few days for emergency services to become available and water is generally the first item that is brought in. The **minimum** preparation for emergency water should be one week. That would be 7 gallons per person as a minimum to store in your home.

What Containers Should I Use?

You should only store water in food-grade plastic containers with tight-fitting screw-on caps. You can purchase new containers if you desire. All used storage containers must be thoroughly washed, sanitized, and rinsed before filling with water for storage. Wash containers with dish soap and rinse thoroughly with clean water. You can sanitize additionally if desired by swishing a solution of 1 teaspoon of liquid household chlorine bleach to a quart of water on all interior surfaces of the container. Rinse the container thoroughly again with clean water before you fill it with storage water.

My wife buys apple juice and orange juice in large hard plastic containers. When we have finished drinking the juice she will clean

the container as described and fill it with storage water. We have many containers filled with water stored on shelves and in various places in our home. We write the month and year on each bottle with a felt pen. Generally you can have confidence that if food was stored in a particular container it is food grade plastic. Be sure to thoroughly clean each container especially well!

You should not store your water in glass containers as there is an inherent risk of breakage. You should not use milk containers for water storage they are not designed for long-term use. Whatever you choose to store water in you should place it out of the sunlight, especially if you have

clear containers. If you need to store your water outside or in the sunlight, it is a good idea to use the blue water containers that will keep the sunlight from penetrating the container.

What Water Should I Use?

Most public water supplies are chlorinated and are safe to store with no additional treatment. In this case adding extra chlorine for long-term storage will be your choice. If you choose to add chlorine to your stored water, use only non-scented bleach. Do not use bleaches with soaps, scents or colors added. Use the following guidelines for storage of a culinary source or public utility:

- Two drops bleach per quart
- Four drops bleach per 2-quart, 2-liter or 1/2 gallon container
- Eight drops bleach per gallon or 4-liter container
- 1 1/8 teaspoons per 5 gallon container
- 2 Tablespoons plus 1 teaspoon for a 55 gallon drum

Once you have added the non-scented bleach to the container, gently agitate or stir. Let it sit for 20-30 minutes before capping.

Vended water is also a good option. Vended water is typically water from the municipality with additional treatment above and beyond that of the municipality. Treat and store this water in the same manner that you would the public utility water.

Where Should I Store My Water?

Store your water in a cool, dry place away from direct sunlight. Heat and light can break down the plastic containers. Also, do not put the water near gasoline or pesticides as the vapors from these products can penetrate the plastic. Your water should be stored on lower shelves that can support the weight. Each gallon of water weighs about 8 pounds. That means that 12 gallons will weigh 100 pounds. Make sure that your shelves can support the weight. Also, it is best to store the water on bottom shelves especially in earthquake prone areas. You can buy one gallon bottles of water that store easily and well.

Store the water under your bed, in your garage or behind your sofa. Put it away and leave it alone. It's for emergency! Once you use it replace it. Always maintain a manageable and adequate level. Use your imagination to find creative places to store your water. It is recommended that you rotate your water. I have heard schedules of 6 months, also one year and two years. Recently I heard of an additive that you could add to your storage water that will make it last at least 5 years. I have not investigated this as of yet. Rotation is your call.

I store several 55 gallon barrels in my garage. You can store four in a row against the wall and put a 2' X 8' piece of plywood on top for a shelf for additional storage. It is simple math; one 55 gallon drum per person per month of emergency water. With that you will have two gallons per person per day, one for eating and drinking and one for hygiene. One thing to remember is getting the water out. Invest in a pump!

My father has had water stored in his basement in liter soda bottles for more than five years. I have tasted it. It is still good. This is not my recommendation! However, I certainly believe that in time of crisis his water will be valuable even with the faint taste of root beer being present.

Some Additional Thoughts

- Store water in several locations around your home and particularly on lower shelves.
- Purchase a hand operated water filter/purifier.
- If you do store water in large drums, store a siphon or pump.
- You can usually find 30-60 gallons of water in the water heater.
- Canned fruits and vegetable also contain water that you can use to hydrate yourself.
- A good rule of thumb is to count a pet as another person: one gallon per pet.
- After a natural disaster, water-borne illnesses appear when the water supply becomes polluted.
- If you buy bottled water, buy an extra case for emergency use. When replacing the water, put the new case on the bottom. You'll always have freshwater for your kit!
- Two-liter soda pop bottles are excellent for water storage.

A Final Water Tip

A five gallon water container can be purchased for $5 to $6. Fill one with water for each member of your family. Now you have 5 days worth of emergency water for you and your family. Put them in a row behind the sofa up against the wall and cover them with a tablecloth, towel or blanket. You will not be caught short. Be sure not to place them near a heat register. A human being can survive three days without water.

Check List Of Items To Consider

- ☐ 55 Gallon Drums (One drum per person per month)
- ☐ 1 Gallon Water Per Person Per Day For Drinking and eating
- ☐ 1 Gallon Water Per Person Per Day For Personal Hygiene
- ☐ Water Pump

Space Blankets Are Out Of This World

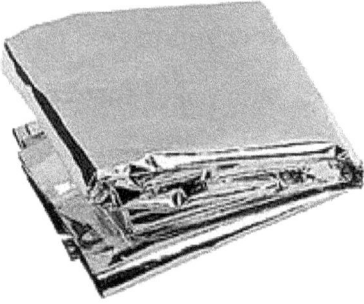

Space blankets are nice but space bags are even better. A space blanket has more uses than just keeping you warm. However, keeping warm in a survival situation should be your first priority.

Three Common Uses:

Blanket – The space blanket's main purpose is helping you stay warm. Wrap the blanket around you to contain your body heat and to break the wind. You can use it for a sleeping bag liner or you can make a simple sleeping bag by placing 2 blankets on top of each other and sealing the edges closed with duct tape.

Shelter - You can use the space blanket as a tent, as a tarp or as a lean-to. It is waterproof and an excellent windbreaker so it will protect you from wind, rain or snow.

The shiny side of the blanket can reflect heat from the sun or from a campfire back to you making you warmer.

Signal for help -- Because the surface of the blanket is reflective, it makes a good signal blanket. Use it to signal across the valley or to an aircraft above for help.

Carry two or three in the glove compartment of your vehicle. They are relatively inexpensive and with some imagination you can find many uses. The reflective characteristics of the Mylar sheet are what you utilize.

How Many Blankets?

Do you have enough blankets? If there is no electricity, then you probably have no heat. If you have no heat it will likely be cold. How many blankets are enough? In Hurricane Sandy the City Of New York passed out 25,000 blankets to those who lost their homes. The nights will be cold in November with no heat. One blanket will **not** be enough!

It would be a good idea to have one warm sleeping bag per person in your household. Consider buying matching bags that can zip together. Three or four children can keep warn in this double bag.

You can line your sleeping bag with additional blankets. You can put on a pair or two of socks. I have a couple of pairs of wool socks and will wear them over my cotton socks in the winter.

To be sure you have enough blankets to keep warm I suggest that you sit on your porch, outside, in the cold evening. Wrap up for about 15 minutes you will find out quickly if you have enough blankets. You should have three to four warm blankets for each person in your house.

Understand that if you have no heat, then in time, the temperature inside and outside will eventually equalize. A good pair of sweatpants and a sweatshirt can give added warmth to any sleeping bag. The good news is that in the house you will be out of the wind and weather. So the question you need to answer here is: How many blankets will you need?

Suggestion: Get some extra blankets from garage sales and secondhand stores. Store them in re-sealable plastic bags so they will be clean when you need them.

Check List Of Items To Consider

- ☐ Sleeping Bag For Each Person
- ☐ Blankets
- ☐ Space Blankets
- ☐ Space Bags
- ☐ Duct Tape
- ☐ Sweatpants And Sweatshirt
- ☐ Wool Socks

"Poor-Boy" Emergency Power

For less than $1000 you can provide emergency power!

When the power is out nothing will work! You have no lights. You cannot cook. Your furnace will not work. And you are left alone in the cold dark night. Having the right size generator is very important. The following tips and information should help you be successful with that task.

What You Need...

First: A 3,500 to 5,000 watt generator should generally be sufficient. These generators can typically be purchased from $300 to $500. A 3500 watt generator will use 1/3 to 1/2 gal/hr of fuel. A 5000 watt will use 3/4 to 1 gal/hr. Fuel consumption is critical because fuel may be limited. Your generator must also have a 240 Volt 30Amp outlet. The 240 V requirement will power up both sides of your electrical panel. If you use a 120 V generator only half the breakers on your panel will be able to work. You can certainly use a 120 V generator. However, the circuits that you want to work may not be the ones that are hot. If this is your option then get help to put the circuits you need to use in the side that works.

Second: A custom-made male/male extension cord to connect the generator to your house must be fabricated by a competent fabricator. Naturally the plug ends should match your generator and your wall plug. **CAUTION:** *Never plug this cord into a generator unless it is plugged into the wall first. The main power must be turned off or the male end could be hot and therefore becomes a dangerous, exposed live wire.*

Third: if you do not have a 240 Volt 30Amp outlet you must also install a 220 Volt wall outlet somewhere near your main power shut off. This is to connect the male/male cord from your house to your generator. This is the interface between the power supply (the generator) and the appliance (the house).

How it works...

Think of your house as a large appliance with many switches and appliances. To make it work you must plug it into a power supply, either the Power Company or your generator. Your house can only receive power from one source at a time. Since you are connected to the Power Company you must turn off (disconnect) the main switch before you connect your house to the generator. With no possibility of power being fed to your house you can now plug your house into the running generator. I cannot stress how important it is to have help to do this correctly. Electricity can be very dangerous!

Even if the power is off you must switch the main breaker off to avoid power feed when power is restored. Not doing this properly will damage your generator. You could also be sending your power up the line and possible endangering others. There is great danger in back-feeding power up the line.

A Few Important Points...

- Only run your generator when you absolutely need power. Remember that you are using gasoline that may be rationed or unavailable.

- Turn off all lights, appliances, TV's and other items that are always on or on standby. It may be easier to just unplug these items.

- Refrigerator and freezers do not need continual power to keep food. Keep the doors closed.

- Running your generator 30 to 45 minutes three or four times a day should be sufficient for all your needs and save you precious fuel.

- Remember that this is "Emergency" power; only use what you absolutely need.

- Use the table at the end of this section to determine your needs and to plan for efficient usage.

- Run your generator for a few minutes every two or three months.

- Turn the fuel off and let the generator run out of fuel when finished. An empty carburetor can help avoid sediment from building up in the carburetor.

- As a last resort a qualified electrician can pull the meter to safely back feed power to the house.

Make An Illustrated Instruction Card

Make an illustrated card with step-by-step details on how to start-up your back-up power. Make photos of the actual items to make identification easy. Laminate the card and attach it to your generator. Below is a sample.

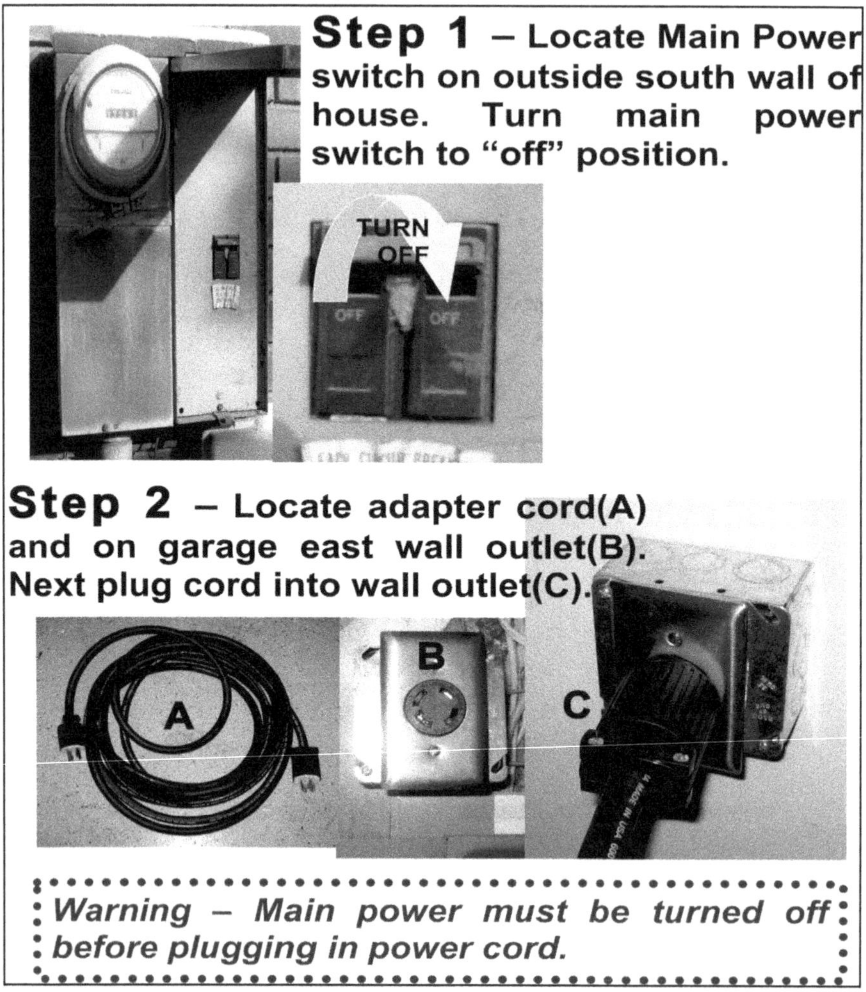

Step 1 – Locate Main Power switch on outside south wall of house. Turn main power switch to "off" position.

TURN OFF

Step 2 – Locate adapter cord(A) and on garage east wall outlet(B). Next plug cord into wall outlet(C).

B
A
C

Warning – Main power must be turned off before plugging in power cord.

It is a good idea to start your generator every two to three months to check the operation and change the oil at least annually. You should consider also storing an extra sparkplug, oil and gasoline. This is an example of the proceedure card that I put together for one of my brothers. It is specific for his home.

Step 3 – Make sure all major appliances extra lights and small appliances are turned off in house. Now you can start generator and let it warm up. Plug in adapter cord to generator. Switch toggle to 240 Volts.

TIPS – Use only necessary items in an emergency. To conserve fuel run generator :30 to :45 minutes 3 or four times a day to keep fridge and freezer cold. Use small appliances during above intervals to maximize efficiency. Also plan intervals during news times for added efficiency.

NOTICE – If generator bogs down and dies then the power demand is too great for the generator. Be sure you have turned off all appliances, lights and electrical items that draw power. If the problem persists go to you electrical panel and turn off all breakers except generator breaker (Stove breaker top left). First turn on fridge, then freezer, next heater. Continue to turn on all 120V single breakers. If one stops generator then that breaker has the big demand. You may need to leave it off until power is back on or reduce the load by unplugging the appliance.

Must stay ON

When Power comes back on:
1 – Turn off generator
2 – Unplug adapter cord
3 – Turn main power on outside
4 – Turn on any breakers you turned off

Important Warning!

<u>There is innate danger in any electrical installation. If you do not have ample electrical understanding then seek help from a competent electrician.</u>

The information in the following table will help you determine the most efficient use of the appliances you would like to use. It is important not to overload the generator. It will not function properly when overloaded.

When using several appliances at the same time, stagger the start to put less demand on the generator. The start-up load is always greater than the running load. Turn all the breakers off that you will not be using. This will ensure that you will not turn on the unwanted items and power hogs accidentally. Do not turn on the breakers for the air conditioner, the range or the electric dryer.

Check List Of Items To Consider

☐ Generator   ☐ Special Cord

☐ 220 Volt Outlet   ☐ Illustrated Start-up Card

How Much Power Do You Need?

Appliance	Running	Startup
Dishwasher	700	1400
Electric Skillet	1600	
Electric Range Single	2100	
Microwave	600-1200	900-1800
Refrigerator/Freezer	700	2000
Washing machine	1200	2400
Clothes dryer**	5800	1800
Lights	See bulb	
Radio	50-200	
TV	300	
Furnace		
1/6 HP	500	750
1/4 HP	600	1000
1/3 HP	700	1400
1/2 HP	875	2350
Central Air**		
Computers		
Desktop	600-800	
Laptop	200-250	
Monitor	200-250	
Fax	600-800	
Printer	400-600	

*All ratings are estimates

**Power hogs, best not used

See plate on motor showing Amps and Volts, multiply Amps x Volts and that equals your Wattage: Amps X Volts = Watts

Sanitation

Here is an inexpensive and practical answer to emergency potty needs. This grab-n-go sanitation system is totally self-contained and is always ready for use.

While studying the aftermath of hurricane Sandy I read a troubling headline that referred to tenants "Defecating in the hallways." With no water, toilets will not be working. If you are forced outside you will need facilities for sanitation needs. Don't count on the government or relief organizations to take care of you. You will be disappointed. Plan ahead and you will have just what you need to be prepared!

The Port-A-Potty Bucket

Take a 6 or 5 gallon bucket (6 gallon best for adults because of the extra height). Buckets can be purchased at hardware stores. Also most large markets have

companies that sell containers to manufactures that should have exactly what you need.

Next line the bucket with a plastic bag (opaque is best). You want a bag that is large enough to completely fill the bucket and the bag should be resting on the bottom of the bucket.

Now attach the toilet seat to the top of the bucket holding the bag in place. This potty lid is purchased for about $10. You can find them at camping and sporting goods stores or order on the Internet.

If you do not use a liner in the bucket (not recommended) just dispose of waste as needed. However, keep in mind that you will then need to wash out the bucket each time.

To absorb moisture sprinkle a small amount of kitty litter into the waste bag. Add more kitty litter as needed. Tie the bag closed and dispose. Kitty litter and chemicals will allow you to go longer between disposals.

MORE:

You can use RV treatment chemicals and RV toilet paper for quicker breakdown and odor control. Chemicals will allow you to go longer between cleanups.

Without chemicals you can add wood ashes to the bucket. This will help with smell and promote decay. Ashes are readily available at any campfire.

I fill my potty bucket with supplies and have it ready and stored in my preparedness area for quick access in an emergency. As pictured earlier you can see that I store inside my bucket several rolls of toilet paper, a roll of plastic bags, hand sanitizer and a plastic jar filled with kitty litter. Again, this is always inside the bucket, grab-n-go! No pun intended!

For hygiene I add a bottle or two of hand sanitizer. You can also use sanitary wipes for your hands. You have likley used these products before. They are available in almost any store and they do a great job. Be sure to have extra to use to generally clean your hands at other times like when preparing food.

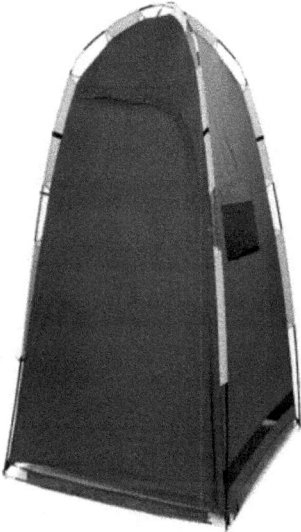

For privacy you can make a tarp enclosure. To do this you will need a tarp and some rope. You can also purchase a shower tent as shown. These tents are available for less than $50. Be sure to store the tent with your survival toilet for easy access.

In A Pinch:

There are other ways to collect and dispose of potty waste. If you are in your home without services, you can use your commode to simulate the Port-A-Potty bucket. Secure a bag to the lid to collect the waste. You should then share the tip with other tenants to keep the problem out of the hall.

Before disposing of the waste, seal the bag. If it is completely sealed there will be no odor. Dispose of the bag in the proper designated area and be careful not to puncture the bag! If solid waste **is** not dealt with quickly and properly serious health issues will develop. Be aware that there is always a great risk of fecal contamination in these situations. Wash your hands after handling any waste.

One More Option:

Dig a latrine, yes, a good old fashioned outhouse. Dig a hole in which to bury the waste. Cover the waste with a thin layer of dirt to keep the smell and flies down. Always clean your hands with soap and water or a hand cleaner for safety. Constructing a latrine is not complicated but you will need a shovel and eventually some toilet paper.

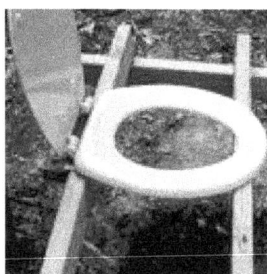

You may need to be creative and resourceful to provide sanitary toilet services in an emergency. Remove a toilet seat and build a comfortable latrine area. Make sure that the shovel and a pile of dirt are easily available to cover the waste.

This option assumes that you will have a shovel to dig the hole and bury the waste. It is extremely important to bury the waste. Cleanliness and hygiene are critical to successful survival of any disaster. Health hazards can develop quickly. With a little preplanning, acquisition of supplies, storing resources properly, and knowing how to correctly use them the severity of the disaster will be greatly reduced.

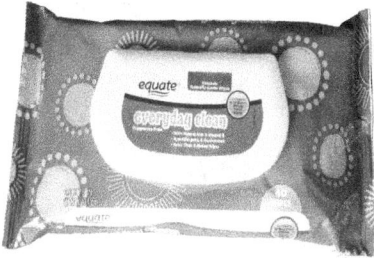

I cannot emphasize enough the dangers of fecal contamination. Sanitation will keep away lots of illness. Make sure that your toilet facilities are a safe distance from your living and eating areas. And always wash your hands when finished and especially before preparing food. Maintain a supply of wet wipes and hand sanitizer to enhance personal sanitation!

Check List Of Items To Consider

☐ 5 or 6 Gallon Bucket   ☐ Kitty Litter

☐ Toilet Lid   ☐ Shovel

☐ Toilet Paper   ☐ Shower Tent

☐ Hand Sanitizer   ☐ Wet Wipes

Emergency Cooking--- Indoors And Out!

I recommend this butane stove as perhaps the best universal option for emergency cooking. The stove is easy to use and is totally self-contained. The Piezo-Electric igniter eliminates the need for matches. This stove can be used both indoors and outdoors.

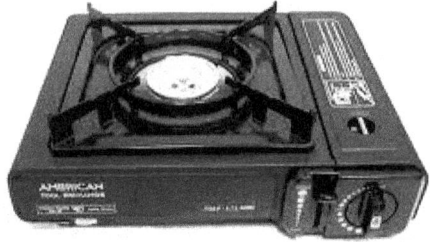

CAUTION: The stove is not a heater and should only be used for cooking.

This stove is available at most Asian markets and can be purchased for less than $20.00. They can also be purchased online for about $25.00 with shipping. Just search: "butane stove."

The butane canisters nestle into the side compartment of the stove and are also a bargain at the Asian Market. One canister will provide fuel for several meals depending on cook time. You would do well to practice with a few simple meals that you will prepare in crisis before putting your stove away for an emergency.

Each canister contains 220g of butane. The stove has a maximum rating of 7,650 Btu/Hr. with a maximum fuel consumption on high of 160g/hr. The heat output of this stove is roughly equal to the large burner on high of most electric ranges. One canister should then last about 1.25 hours on high and butane will store indefinitely. The Asian market I go to sells the fuel at four canisters for $5.00. That breaks down to $1.25 per canister.

One morning I used this stove to make pancakes and scrambled eggs in my kitchen. When I finished I weighed the canister to determine my fuel usage. The morning meal consumed 50g of fuel. With 220g per canister that meant that I used about 20% of a canister. Cooking the same 20 minutes for each meal would mean that you would be able to cook at least five meals with one canister. If you just boil water for noodles or heat a can of soup or stew, you will use less fuel and the canister will last even longer.

I recommend that you store your stove in a box with a few fuel canisters, add a pot and a few packs of Ramen Noodles, or other

easy to prepare canned foods. You should also store some plates, bowls and utensils with your stove. You can pick up some used items at the second hand store or use some of the odd items that you have at home. Store it somewhere that is easy to find. Be sure that when you use your kit that you always replace the items used so to always be ready for the next event. You are now ready to grab and go or survive at home with no utilities.

Find some food that can be easily prepared to keep in your kit. If you have canned goods you may need a manual can opener. Remember that you are preparing a

kit that will allow you to survive until aid arrives in a few days. Simple but adequate is the rule of thumb.

Three keys to success in surviving any emergency are:

1. Have what you need.

2. Know how to use what you have.

3. Keep it easily accessible.

Don't be caught short! Make a plan and follow your plan!

Check List Of Items To Consider

☐ Cooking Pot

☐ Frying Pan

☐ Plates

☐ Bowls

☐ Knife, Fork and Spoon

☐ Canned Food

☐ Dried Soups

☐ Ramen Noodles

☐ Manual Can Opener

☐ _____

☐ _____

☐ _____

☐ _____

Mini Toilet Paper Roll

Have you ever needed some toilet paper and found there was none or possibly got caught out in nature and Mother Nature came calling? What do you do? It is somewhat awkward to keep a whole roll of toilet paper in the glove compartment. Dragging a large roll of toilet paper with you wherever you go can also be embarrassing.

I offer you the perfect solution, which I have done this for years. Keep an eye on the roll of toilet paper in your bathrooms. When the role is largely used up and there is about one half of an inch of paper left on the roll change it out for a new one. Now you have a small role that is convenient to use.

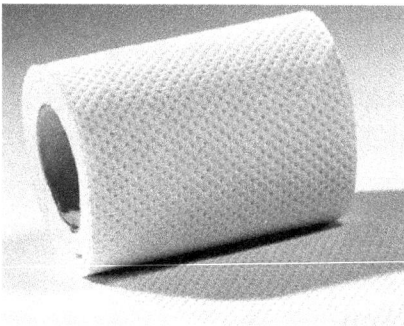

I take it one step further. I put it in a Ziploc bag and press it flat. It will always stay clean in the plastic bag and will not get torn up in the glove compartment or elsewhere. When it is pushed flat it will work just as well as before. However it stores so much more conveniently. Now it will fit easily into a purse, a glove compartment or the pocket of your jacket.

Start building your private stash of mini toilet paper rolls. Once you start having them available and see how convenient they are, you will find many additional uses. Before long, you will have them stashed in many emergency places.

Put a mini-roll in all your 72 hour kits. Put several in your camping supplies. Keep one in your car. You will find many places and uses for your mini TP rolls.

Check List Of Items To Consider

- ☐ Zip Lock Bags
- ☐ Toilet Paper Mini Rolls

Earthquake Proof Your House

- Secure large appliances to a wall stud using bolts and plumber's tape to secure refrigerators, water heaters and ovens.

- Fasten televisions, stereos and computer monitors.

- Put heavy objects on lower shelves. In an earthquake falling objects cause the most injuries.

- Store hazardous and flammable fluids away from potentially explosive appliances such as gas dryers, gas ranges and gas water heaters.

- Store chemicals in sealed containers on a low shelf.

- Affix decorative items to their locations with poster putty

- Attach latches to cabinet doors to prevent items from falling out.

- Anchor large fixtures such as bookshelves, cabinets, dressers and china hutches. You can use the plumber's tape or you can purchase special fastening straps that are particularly designed for anchoring large fixtures to the studs in the wall.

- Position your beds away from potential hazards such as windows, pictures hanging on the wall and ceiling fans.

- Move items that are hanging above couches or chairs such as: mirrors; framed artwork; other items that can fall on someone sitting there.
- Learn how to turn off the utilities.
- Have a 72 hour kit ready to use if you are ordered to evacuate.

Check List Of Items To Consider

☐ Plumbers Tape

☐ Poster Putty

☐ Appliance Anchors

☐ Cabinet Door Handles

☐ Survey Your House For Problems

Protect Valuables From Water Damage

Here are a few ideas to help you earthquake proof your home. This list is by no means exhaustive. It is meant to be a starting point. It is meant to get you thinking. You are required to take action.

As I have watched several flooding situations I have seen the property of many people get destroyed. Not only basements flooded but also main levels from flood surges, mountain snow runoff, and even torrential rainstorms. People often have a short time to prepare and are left to the mercy of Mother Nature. However, in many cases there was some warning. Flood warnings are issued. River cresting's are mentioned as to how much and when. Storm surges are predicted with great accuracy. People often have time to prepare. With supplies on hand and an emergency plan in place losses can be reduced.

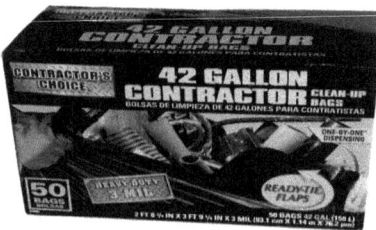

One day while walking in my shop, I noticed some "contractor trash bags." These are heavy-duty bags at least 40 to 50 gallons per bag. My mind turned to hurricane

Sandy and the great personal losses of precious memories. What if the flood victims had sealed items they wanted to protect in one of these heavy duty, airtight bags? Thus this tip was developed.

Heavy-duty bags are available in up to 65 gallons and even larger. Some are clear, some are black but the color doesn't matter. The more heavy duty the bag the better chance they have of withstanding the disaster. 2mm is great however 3mm is best. I looked at my supply of large garbage bags. They are 2mm, 30 gallon size and clear. I put them in a bag, leaving the bag mostly full of air, twisted the top closed. The top was then folded over and sealed with a tight rubber band. I then put light pressure on the top of the bag to see if it was airtight. It was! Be sure you do a good job sealing the bags.

Now here is my tip: carefully put into the bags precious items that might get flooded. Be careful not to puncture the bags! Next carefully press most of the air out of the bag. Seal the bag by twisting the top tightly then fold the top over. Finally put a rubber band to hold the bag closed. For adding strength to the seal you can put some duct tape over the rubber band.

To be prepared make sure you have these three things: a box of large heavy-duty bags; large rubber bands; and some duct tape or packaging tape. A box of 50 heavy-duty 50 gallon bags will cost between $20 and $25 and can be purchased at any hardware store or home center. They have both 2mil and 3 mil thickness of bags. Don't use twist ties. Use a rubber band and put several loops around your fold to help keep it closed better. Don't be afraid to use several rubber bands for added security. These are your valuables!

Once you have your bags filled you can put them in the closet. Close the door so they won't be thrown around. Also you could position them somewhere else where they might be protected from being moved around.

This is an inexpensive way to with any luck protect your valuables. Unless you have the items needed before you need them then this tip has little value.

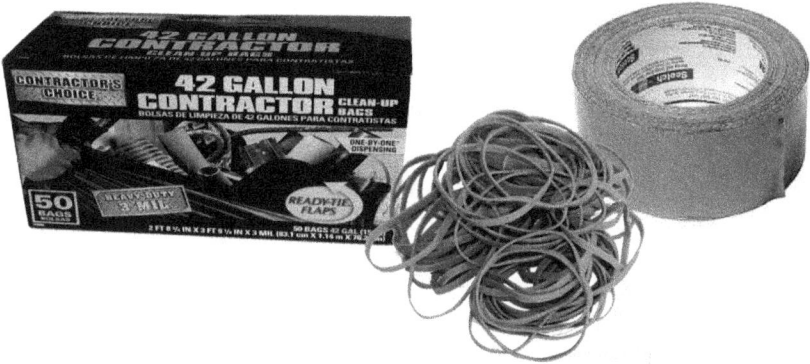

Check List Of Items To Consider

☐ Contractor Bags   ☐ Rubber Bands

☐ Duct Tape

What About Cash?

Money is purely an arbitrary means of exchange. You can buy anything if you have enough money to sway the seller. Bartering is the purest way of selling goods and services. If you have what somebody wants and they have something you want it is easy to make an exchange and both will likely come out with a good deal.

In crisis don't be afraid to exchange goods and services to obtain what you need. So in an emergency you may be exchanging a can of tuna fish for a gallon of water. I would only assume that such a scenario would not happen unless there was a mega-crisis with little to no services for an extended period of time.

Nevertheless, in a crisis you need to have some cash on hand. There will likely be items that you need and a little cash can likely solve the issue. When the power is out the ATM's will not work. The banks and many businesses will also be closed. It is said, "Cash is king!" In our ATM society we need to have an alternative--- cash on hand.

Store a total of $20, $50 or $100. Only you know how much you should have available. Keep it always safely put away. Keep reminding yourself why you put it away and don't spend it! It is put away for an emergency. It doesn't need to be a large amount and you might never use any of it. But just like any of the preparedness items that you store for an emergency they become very valuable when you need them, but only if you have them.

Storing small bills is best. This is just in case you may not be able to get change. Have some one's some five's and some ten's. Put them in an envelope seal it and mark it emergency preparedness. Put it with your 72 hour kits.

A few words of caution, however. It is not wise to let others know that you have money. If you were carrying the cash with you I would recommend that you put it in 2 or 3 pockets. If someone were to see you take cash from one pocket subsequently grabs it from you, you would not have lost everything.

There are those who would suggest you have gold and silver, yes, precious metals. This can be a good idea however you must consider a few items:

1. The value of the coin or your precious metal denomination may be too much to make an exchange.

2. Old silver coins, commonly referred to as "junk silver," are an inexpensive way to have emergency money in the form of precious metals.

3. The nice feature of precious metal in coin form is that it can be put away in your preparedness storage and the value will generally stay favorable.

I suggest you take some time to study and determine if precious metals and which ones are right for you. You should also determine how much and what quantities. Do not solely rely on cash and do not solely rely on precious metals. Once again keep in mind that money is an arbitrary means of exchange. What are you willing to give for what you want to receive? Food and water may very well become the most valuable.

Check List Of Items To Consider

- ☐ Small Bills In An envelope
- ☐ Research Precious Metals

Learn CPR

My daughter, a schoolteacher, and a couple of her friends saved a drowned child. It was her CPR training put into action that saved the life. She and her friends were playing volleyball and heard screams at the pool. They ran to the poolside and saw a mother screaming as her child floated on top of the water. They pulled the child out and immediately began CPR.

Someone yelled, "Call 911." It was not long until the baby was spitting up and crying. Had it not been for the fast action of someone who knew CPR the child would not have survived. This story repeats itself all too often in our daily lives.

CPR is not hard to learn. Just think about it for a minute. The person has stopped breathing. Their heart has stopped beating. If you attempt CPR you may save a life.

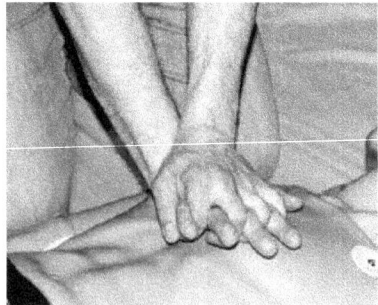

There are many stories of people who have done just that and expressed that their only CPR training was from watching TV. Just try! But better yet, take time to learn CPR!

There are many places that will teach you CPR. The **Red Cross** has classes along with other community resources. There are some very good instructional videos on the Internet that you can watch and acquire some knowledge. I am certain that your City Hall or local paramedics can tell you where you can get CPR training locally. CPR on a child is different than that on an adult. So set a goal to learn CPR and get trained!

Set a goal to learn CPR and take a friend! The live saved could be your own.

Check List Of Items To Consider

- ☐ Research Where to Learn CPR
- ☐ Lean CPR
- ☐ Become Certified

Don't forget the pets!

My daughter and her husband often visit us with their oversized dog. She will always bring two stainless steel bowls, one for water and one for food. She also brings a Ziploc bag full of dog food. Finally she brings a chain to restrain the dog in the back of our property if necessary.

Whatever your pet, whatever the size, you can do the same. The principle is simple. Have a Ziploc bag full of food. If you use canned food have enough for 3 to 5 days and a manual can opener if necessary. Add to your stash one bowl for water and one bowl for food. Place all of the items in another large Ziploc bag, box or container of some sort. It is that simple. Store it in a convenient place, rotate your food and replace what you use immediately. Always be ready to leave quickly.

Also you need to have a supply of plastic bags to retrieve the animal's poop. Some areas may not allow pets. Size of your pets may also be an issue at some facilities. My best advice is to plan in advance where you will go with your pets. Explore several options today to have the answer before the problem arises.

If you have more than one pet prepare individual emergency ration bags for each one. Keep in mind that you may have to take them to separate locations.

Check List Of Items To Consider

- ☐ Food and Water Bowls
- ☐ Plastic Poop Bags
- ☐ Leash
- ☐ Chain
- ☐ Sleeping Bed/Mat

Sprouting, Natures Secret

Here is an amazing way to have fresh vegetables for your salad! Learn how to grow your own sprouts. Follow this process and you can have fresh sprouts on a regular basis. When sprouting you need to remember that it typically takes 6 or 7 days before you can harvest your sprouts.

Choose a handful of sprouts that you like. Not all sprouts are created equal! Once again, I urge you to become familiar with this process. Use sprouts from time to time in your menus. This is about as easy as it gets! Just a mason jar and some seeds is all it takes and you can sprout seeds.

I can recommend Alfalfa seeds, Clover seeds, Radish seeds, Broccoli seeds, Wheat seeds and Pea seeds. This is a well-rounded selection of seeds and you can make a very nutritious sprout salad. These seeds are easy to obtain, easy to sprout and are very agreeable. In time of crisis and you need fresh vegetables, sprouts can be an inexpensive answer. Plus they are very easy to sprout with the ability to add great taste to any meal.

Go to the health food store, organic grocery store or on the internet and buy a small amount of seeds with the thought in mind that you will sprout and use them to be certain that you can do it and that you will eat them. The process is very simple and basically is the same for all sprouts. Be sure you purchase seeds that are for sprouting because garden seeds may be chemically treated.

A quart mason jar is an ideal sprouting container. You will need a lid that water can drain through. A nylon stocking is excellent. A piece of netting or even a piece of cheesecloth will also make an excellent drain cap.

Follow These Three Simple Steps:

Step 1 – Soak Overnight

Place a total of 2 Tablespoons of seeds, mixed or individual in a one-quart Mason jar. Use the ring to attach *Sprouting Screen*. Cover with three times water. Let seeds soak 8-12 hours then pour water off. Peas, lentils and wheat use 1/2 to 3/4 cup of seeds.

Step 2 - Rinse 2 times a day

Rinse twice daily by covering the sprouts with water. Gently swirl water in jar. Drain off all the water after 5-10 minutes. This is just like watering your garden. Repeat this rinse two times each day for 4-6 days. There is no need to expose to direct sunlight yet. (Peas, lentils, wheat)*

Step 3 - De-hull in final rinse

Once you are ready to harvest, place all the sprouts in a bowl of water and gently agitate and separate sprouts and hulls. Let sprouts sit in sunlight for 8-10 hours to chlorophyll-up. The leaves will turn a rich green and increase in nutrition.

*See Sprouting Chart

Enjoy! And keep refrigerated!

Sprouts will last up to two weeks if well drained and stored in the refrigerator. Add peas, lentils and wheat to stews and soups. Use sprouts to garnish salads, sandwiches or just eat straight.

ENJOY SPROUTS!

Endless Uses!

Excellent Nutrition!

Fresh Vegetables!

Sprouting Chart

Seeds	Seeds In Quart Jar	Soaking Time	Days To Harvest	Notes
Wheat*	1 Cup	8-12 Hrs.	2	Harvest when sprout is ½ the length
Alfalfa	2 Tbls.	8-12 Hrs.	6-7	Exposed to sunlight for the last day
Broccoli	2 Tbls.	8-12 Hrs.	6-7	Exposed to sunlight for the last day
Radish	2 Tbls.	8-12 Hrs.	6-7	Exposed to sunlight for the last day
Clover	2 Tbls.	8-12 Hrs.	6-7	Exposed to sunlight for the last day
Peas*	1 Cup	8-12 Hrs.	4	Harvest when 1/3 length of seed
Mung Beans	3 Tbls.	8-12 Hrs.	3-5	Harvest to personal preference 3 to 5 days
Lintel	3 Tbls	8-12 Hrs.	3-4	Harvest when 1/4-1/2" tail

Peas and wheat should sprout until sprout is about 1/3 the length of the seed.

The best part about sprouting is that is very easy and it can be done without special equipment

Some Sprouting Hints:

- For best flavor and nutrition use sprouts within one week.

- Keep harvested sprouts refrigerated.

- Sprouts are an excellent source of vitamin C.

- Green leafy sprouts full of chlorophyll are full of vitamin A.

- Sprouts are easy to digest.

- Sprouts are low in calories and high in fiber.

- Save and re-use the rinsing water.

- Use fresh water for final rinse and to de-hull.

Sprouts can be used in breads, soups, pancakes, omelets, casseroles, meatloaf, salads, or just eaten straight. They can also be used in smoothies and other nutritional drinks. Sprouts are excellent in place of lettuce on a sandwich.

Sprouting is one of nature's best-kept secrets. A preparedness pantry with sprouts will always have healthy options. There is much written about sprouting and you may choose to expand your knowledge. This section is intended to give you some basics with a well-rounded inventory of seeds. The most important thing here is to have a working knowledge and enough seed variety that you will be able to add health and nutrition to your diet. Sprouting is something that you can add to your everyday diet. Begin today and get a head start on preparedness.

Check List Of Items To Consider

- ☐ Large Mouth Quart Mason Jar With Ring
- ☐ Screen
- ☐ Rinsing Bowl
- ☐ Variety Of Seeds
  - o Alfalfa
  - o Wheat
  - o Radish
  - o Broccoli
  - o Mung Beans
  - o Lentils
  - o Clover
  - o Peas
  - o _____
  - o _____
  - o _____
  - o _____
  - o _____

Dutch Oven Emergency Cooking Kit

Here is a grab and go idea that will have your Dutch oven always ready to cook at least three meals. It stores easily and is totally self-contained. I recommend that you have at least two alternative methods to cook a meal. You should be familiar with how to use them.

Dutch oven cooking is an old method of cooking. It is relatively easy and is similar to baking in an oven. The basic concept is that your Dutch oven acts just like an oven. It can produce an even heat basically like your oven at a specific predetermined temperature.

What you will need:

- **12" Dutch Oven.** This is the most efficient size. I own two. They are always filled and ready to go. The deep oven is the best choice.

- **3 Bags Of Briquettes**. Use a one gallon Ziploc bag for 27 briquettes. This can provide a 375°- 12" Dutch Oven and you will have three meals worth. For the third bag, fill the starter can with 27 briquettes then bag it can and all.

- **Matches. Y**ou will need a lighter or matches. I have both. The matches should be strike-anywhere matches that are available at the local grocery store. The lighters are the three for a dollar from the Dollar Store.

- **Lighter Fluid** is purchased at any grocery store and most drug stores. Once you have this unique container you can pry the top off and refill it as needed. Best choices are the 5 oz. or 8 oz. size.

- **Tongs** are needed to handle the hot coals. Make sure that they are small enough to fit in the Dutch oven.

- **Homemade Starter Can.** This can is easily made and works perfect for starting your briquettes. (See: *How To Make A Starter Can*)

- **Cleaning Sponge** is optional

- **A Copy Of The** *"Baking Temperature Chart for Dutch Oven Cooking"* will assist you in achieving the desired temperature in your oven.

Once you have assembled your emergency Dutch oven kit you will always be ready to go. Keep the kit accessible. Consider preparing a Ziploc pouch of dried vegetables and rice for a quick emergency meal. Also see: **Quick And Easy Emergency Recipes.**

Now that you established an alternative cooking method, practice it so you will become proficient in this cooking skill. Use your Dutch oven every month or two to cook a meal. Part of being prepared is knowing how to use what you have.

Baking Temperature Chart for Dutch Oven Cooking

Oven Top/bottom*	325°	350°	375°	400°	425°	450°
8"	15 10/5	16 11/5	17 11/6	18 12/6	19 13/6	20 14/6
10"	19 13/6	21 14/7	23 16/7	25 17/8	27 18/9	29 19/10
12"	23 16/7	25 17/8	27 18/9	29 19/10	31 21/10	33 22/11
14"	30 20/10	32 21/11	34 22/12	36 24/12	38 25/13	40 26/14

*To Bake place 2/3 of the briquettes on the top and 1/3 on the bottom
*To Simmer reverse briquettes to 2/3 on bottom 1/3 on top
*Each briquette will produce about 10° - 15° F. worth of heat

"Rule-of-Thumb" Dutch oven cooking Guidelines

1. One charcoal briquette, or equally sized hot coal, will equate to approx. 10-15 degrees of heat on a fair camping day, (not real cold, rainy, or windy)
2. Generally, to get a 350° inside-oven temperature the number of coals would be 2 times the Dutch oven diameter. e.g. 12" oven = 24 briquettes. (Use a little judgment here, sometimes more - sometimes less)
3. For baking, put twice as many coals on top as under the bottom. For example if your heat range calls for 15 briquettes, then put 10 on top and 5 underneath. To simmer reverse briquettes to 2/3 on bottom 1/3 on top.
4. For even heat, rotate oven and lid 90 degrees in opposite directions approx. halfway through recipe cooking time.
Hot coal amounts are not a set-n-go thing. To maintain desired temperature you will need to replenish coals/briquettes as they burn down.

©2012 Sam Spencer

How To Make A Charcoal Starter Can

1. Start with a 52 oz. can. This will hold 27 briquettes and also fit into the Dutch Oven.

2. Consume the contents of the can. (Soup, tomato or vegetable juice, 4 ¼' Dia. 7" tall.)

3. Wash can and peel off the label.

4. Use a step drill for large holes or a ½" drill bit for smaller holes. Just drill a few more.

5. If the holes are rough then use a round file to de-burr them.

A handy friend can help you drill the holes. You do not need large holes. Even ½" would work. You will just have more. If you only have holes around the bottom of the can, that would also work. The air is drawn through the bottom holes. As the hot air rises it pulls air up through the can and keeps the coals burning well.

This is real easy, very cheap and portable!

Quick And Easy Emergency Recipes

Five Can Chicken and Rice

1 Can Green Beans

1 Can Peas

1 Can Corn

1 Can Cream of Chicken soup

1-2 Cans Chicken

2 Cups Long Grain Rice

1 Quart water

Season as desired.

Pour all ingredients into Dutch oven. Stir occasionally. Cook until rice is done.

This recipe makes about four quarts. That would be at least twenty 6 oz. servings. That's a lot of food!

Mixed Vegetable Stew

    3 cups mixed dried vegetables

    1 Can Cream of Chicken soup

    1-2 Cans Chicken

    3 Quart water

    Season as desired

Pour all ingredients into Dutch oven and stir. Cook until vegetables are soft.

This recipe makes about four quarts of stew. That would be at least twenty 6 oz. servings.

Practice For Preparedness

Gather all the ingredients for your recipes. Put them into a small box so that you can grab and go with your Dutch oven kit. The two recipes above will easily store for several years. One idea is to prepare the recipe that you have stored once or twice a year. This will keep you practiced and you will also rotate your goods. Practice with other recipes to develop the skill of Dutch oven cooking.

Check List Of Items To Consider

- ☐ 12" Dutch oven
- ☐ 3 Bags of briquettes
- ☐ Matches
- ☐ Lighter fluid
- ☐ Tongs
- ☐ Homemade starter can
- ☐ Cleaning Sponge
- ☐ A copy of the *"Baking Temperature Chart for Dutch Oven Cooking"*

Learn To Turn Off Gas, Water And Power

Everyone should know how to turn off the utilities; gas, water and electricity. You should know how to turn them off at the delivery point. The delivery point is typically at the meter and always has a method to shut-off the utility. Most follow a similar pattern. Once you are familiar with them you can easily accomplish this task. Teach family members what natural gas smells like.

Caution: If you turn off the gas for any reason, a qualified professional must turn it back on. NEVER attempt to turn the gas back on yourself.

Natural Gas

Let's start with the gas. Almost all gas meters are the same. A simple adjustable wrench is all you need. The valve is turned 90˙ to open or close. One-quarter turn clockwise to open and one quarter turn counterclockwise to close. When the two holes in the valve are aligned, the gas is

turned off, and a lock can be put in them, the gas is turned off. When the length of the valve is inline with the pipe, the gas is on.

Learning where your gas valve is and how to turn it off is very critical. If you are not sure ask someone who knows, like the landlord. Call your gas company and ask them how. Certainly there is someone you know, like a plumber, who is knowledgeable in this area. Don't be afraid to ask for help!

If you have propane you will turn the valve off at the tank. Treat propane just like natural gas because it is just like natural gas!

Caution: If you turn off the gas for any reason, qualified personnel must turn it back on. The pilot lights must be relit. Care must be taken.

If you smell gas leave immediately and call authorities.

Water

Typically the water meter and shut-off is at the street. The property

owner should know where the valve is. If you cannot find it ask your municipality or water provider to locate it and show you how to turn it off. You may need to clean out some dirt and debris to access and turn the valve. Use a stick to remove spider webs and clean around the valve.

An adjustable wrench or a "T" wrench will do the job. The valve is turned 90˚ to open or close. One-quarter turn clockwise to open and one quarter turn counterclockwise to close. When the two holes in the valve are aligned it is turned off and a lock can be put on.

To help stimulate your memory take photos of the procedure. Print them and keep them available for reference.

Electricity

Electricity can pose a problem. Older homes may not have a shut off main breaker at the meter. It is important that you know where and how to turn the power of. It may be necessary to get some help. My suggestion is that you take enough photos that anyone can easily follow the process. Make a step-by-step card for this process with acrual photos of your application.

Once you have taken the photos of the process design a card that you can print and laminate. Have this card available for easy emergency access and teach other in family to use it. Place it by the breaker box or hang it on the wall beside the power disconnect.

If your home is newer it probably has a main switch. Simply turn the breaker to the off position. If you are not sure then you can always turn all the breakers off at you breaker panel box.

75

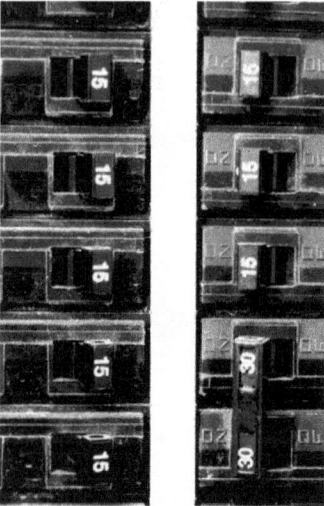

Here is an example of the breaker box. If your house does not have a main breaker to isolate you from the grid or the power company you will need to turn off all the breakers individually.

Once again ask someone who knows and document the process.

Here is an example of the card I made for one of my brothers to instruct him on how to turn the power off at his house. Take time to do the same. Give the card to different

Step 1 – Locate Your Main Power switch on outside west wall of building. Turn main power switch to "off" position.

TURN OFF

51 273 816

163

family members to see if the instructions are easily followed.

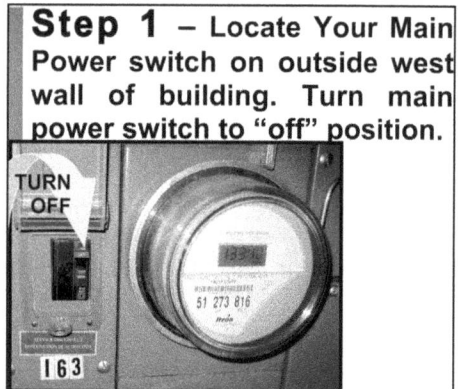

Once again, it may be necessary get help from an electrician and practice beforehand to be sure everyone can do it.

Apartments

If you live in an apartment ask the landlord or superintendent to instruct you how to shut off the utilities for your unit. Take several photographs of the procedure. Then make and print out a card with easy to follow instructions. Keep this card with your emergency preparedness items and easily accessible.

Remember that elevators will not work when the power is out. You will not have heat. Follow some of the tips in this book to ensure that you are warm and can take care of yourself.

Check List Of Items To Consider

- ☐ "T" wrench for water
- ☐ Adjustable Wrench
- ☐ Photos Of Procedure
- ☐ Photos Of Locations of Valves And Breakers

Fuel In A Crisis

After Hurricane Sandy gasoline was impossible to obtain. When there is no power the gas pumps will not work. When a gas station was able to pump gas it was because they had backup power or that power had been restored. Long lines formed and gasoline was rationed. This problem persisted for a couple of weeks.

The power was out for several days. In fact, most people did not see power return for more than a week. There were a few who did not get power back for more than a month. Our dependency on oil is not the problem. We will always have interruptions in supply. The problem is preparedness, the ability to successfully handle an interruption. With planning and preparation you can preempt the problem with solving it beforehand.

When I watched the news reports of people standing in long lines with their gas cans my first question was, "Where did they get the gas cans?" I wondered if they had them stored in their apartments, their garages, or in their cars. I then began to wonder about the many people who did not even have a gas can stored in some corner awaiting just such an emergency.

Obviously then, a gas can is a must for survival preparedness. This does not mean that you have to store a container that is full of gasoline in your house, apartment or garage. The container can certainly be stored empty. Also it is not a fire hazard until you fill the container with fuel.

Another thing to keep in mind is that 5 gallons of gasoline will weigh almost 50 pounds and that is a lot of weight to carry back to where you have your car parked. An easier solution would be to have two 2 1/2 gallon containers for gasoline. Each container will weigh approximately 25 pounds when full. It is much easier to carry 25 pounds in each hand a long distance than to drag 50 pounds the same distance.

A very simple solution would be to purchase two 2 1/2 gallon containers and store them away for an emergency. You can keep them in the back of your car, empty, ready to fill. This is an excellent place to store them since the gasoline will most likely go into the car in which they are stored. If you own several cars consider putting one container in each vehicle. Also, if someday you run out of gasoline the can is in your trunk ready to fill.

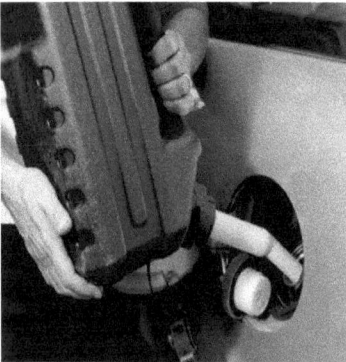

If your situation allows, it is a good idea always have at least one 5 gallon container full of gasoline that is safely stored. You can rotate the fuel every few months by putting it into your vehicle and filling it up again. There are additives that you can put in the fuel that you store to extend its life.

It is also a good idea to keep your gas tank at least half full. When you know that danger is coming it would also be a good idea to periodically top off your tank to be better prepared. If gasoline is being rationed it is wise to always take what is yours. You can also consider using the buddy system: you and a neighbor can team up to carry the rationed fuel back to your respective vehicles, taking turns to fill each container.

Check List Of Items To Consider

- ☐ 5 Gallon Gas Can
- ☐ 2 ½ Gallon Gas Can

Know How To Change A Tire

I was on a business trip with two associates. Jose was driving and blew a tire while doing a "U" turn. We pulled over and then I found out that neither of the men had ever changed a tire on any car nor did they have any idea how to do it.

I asked if they knew where the spare tire and tools were. Again neither had any idea. I soon found all that was needed and promptly changed the tire. In ten minutes we were on our way again. Had I not been there the two young men would have had a great deal of trouble getting the help they needed.

I have taught all of my daughters to change a tire. This training has paid off as they too have educated

82

others who had no idea how to change their tire.

A jack is needed to raise the tire off the ground. The vehicle needs to be raised until the wheel clears the ground and can be turned freely. The jack should be placed securely under the frame of the vehicle.

Next you need a lug wrench to remove the nuts that hold the tire to the hub. Most vehicles use the smaller "doughnut" tire. Replace the damaged tire with the spare and you are on your way!

Check List Of Items To Consider

- ☐ Car Jack
- ☐ Lug Wrench
- ☐ Pad To Kneel On

Communication

"What We Have Here Is A Failure To Communicate!" This is my favorite line from the movie "Cool Hand Luke" starring Paul Newman and George Kennedy. Good communication is extremely vital for success in any situation. This is especially true when we are in a crisis. Good communication will save lives. It can warn of impending danger and it can calm the troubled soul.

In any emergency there is an inherent need to want to know what is going on. You want to know what the dangers are as they relate to you. You want to know if you can travel and when. You want to know when help will arrive. Above all you want to know that your family and loved ones are safe. There is always the need for continued and good communication.

Cellphones have become indispensable. It seems that everyone has one now days. If the power goes out however, the cell towers will not operate. No calling. No texting.

In an emergency there are some recommended practices by the FCC that we should follow:

- Limit non-emergency phone calls. This will minimize network congestion, free up "space" on the network for emergency communications and conserve battery power if you are using a wireless phone;

- Keep all phone calls brief. If you need to use a phone, try to use it only to convey vital information to emergency personnel and/or family;

- For non-emergency calls, try text messaging, also known as short messaging service (SMS) when using your wireless phone. In many cases text messages will go through when your call may not. It will also help free up more "space" for emergency communications on the telephone network;

- If possible try a variety of communications services if you are unsuccessful in getting through with one. For example, if you are unsuccessful in getting through on your wireless phone, try a messaging capability like text messaging or email. Alternatively, try a landline phone if one is available. This will help spread the communications demand over multiple networks and should reduce overall congestion;

- Wait 10 seconds before redialing a call. On many wireless handsets, to re-dial a number, you simply push "send" after you've ended a call to redial the previous number. If you do this too quickly, the data from the handset to the cell sites do not have enough time to clear before you've resent the same data. This contributes to a clogged network;

- Have charged batteries and car-charger adapters available for backup power for your wireless phone;

- Maintain a list of emergency phone numbers in your phone;

- If in your vehicle, try to place calls while your vehicle is stationary;

- Have a family communications plan in place. Designate someone out of the area as a central contact, and make certain all family members know who to contact if they become separated;

- If you have Call Forwarding on your home number, forward your home number to your wireless number in the event of an evacuation. That way you will get incoming calls from your landline phone;

- After the storm has passed, if you lose power in your home, try using your car to charge cell phones or listen to news alerts on the car radio. But be careful – don't try to reach your car if it is not safe to do so, and remain vigilant about carbon monoxide emissions from your car if it is a closed space, such as a garage.

- Tune-in to broadcast and radio news for important news alerts.

Another option is the two-way radio. You can purchase a couple of radios with charges and headsets for less than $30. The less expensive models will have less of a range however. If you step up to the $50 category where you can get a transmission range of up to 35 miles. Range varies based on terrain.

I have four households of family members living within four miles of my house. This is the perfect back-up system for emergency communication. Have one for each member of your family. Teach them to use them and practice. Keep fresh batteries available for replacement. These radios can also be used for vacations and outings for additional communication and safety.

Check List Of Items To Consider

☐ Two-Way Radios   ☐ Chargers   ☐ Extra Batteries

Water Purification

Your best option is stored emergency water or bottled water. When it's not available you must know how to treat contaminated water. Just another reason to store water, as you never know what kind of an emergency you will be surprised with.

Water Filters:

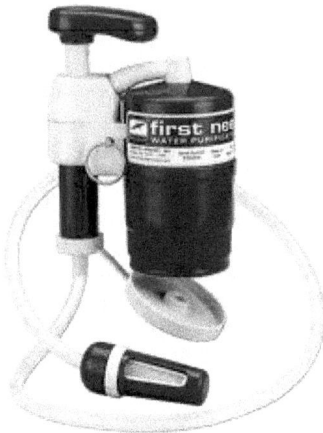

There are several excellent choices in water filters used for emergency and camping. You can purchase an inexpensive camping filter that removes giardia for about $25. It is found in most sporting goods departments and sporting goods stores. Other filters of better quality will cost from $50 to $100. Of course the price continues to climb with name brand, quality and features. Remember that this is an emergency item and it probably will have limited use but it is essential when in an emergency situation.

Chlorine:

Here are some guidelines for adding bleach to your water: Add 16 drops (1/8 teaspoon) of non-scented liquid chlorine bleach to each gallon of collected water. Stir or gently swirl. Let stand 30 minutes. If there is the smell of chlorine it is okay to use. If there is no smell of chlorine you must add an additional 16 drops (1/8 teaspoon) of non-scented liquid chlorine bleach to each gallon of collected water. Let it stand another 30 minutes. If after adding a second treatment of bleach you still cannot smell chlorine then throw away the water and find a better water source.

Boiling Water:

If the water you are treating needs some filtering to remove solid particulates you can use coffee filters or a cloth. Fill a jar with the water to be boiled and let it sit so the solids will settle to the bottom. Once the solids have settled, gently pour off the water trying not to disturb the sediment at the bottom.

Now you can bring the water to a rolling boil (that means big bubbles) for about one full minute. This should kill the bacteria. Once the water has cooled you can pour the water back and forth between two clean containers to improve its taste before drinking it.

If your municipality issues a "Boil Order" for your water, you need to be sure and use the boiled water for the following purposes:

- Brushing teeth
- Cooking
- Preparing drinks
- Drinking
- Washing raw foods or foods in general
- Making ice
- Water for pets

Typically the water is safe for washing dishes, but hot soapy water should be used. Add one tablespoon of bleach per gallon as a precaution. Dishes should be rinsed in boiled water. There are no restrictions on doing laundry and the water should be safe for bathing. If your municipality has lifted the "Boil Order" there are a few precautions to follow after the order is lifted. You need to flush the lines to remove the contaminated water.

- Flush water lines by running all cold water faucets in the home for a couple of minutes.
- Flush automatic icemakers by discarding the next three batches of ice made.
- Run water softeners through a regeneration cycle.
- Run drinking water faucets or fountains for a couple of minutes.
- Run water through all other water connections for five minutes.

Caution: Don't use floodwater as it may be contaminated with toxic chemicals such as gasoline, pesticides and other contaminates. Do not even attempt to treat floodwater.

REMEMBER: Err on the side od caution!

Check List Of Items To Consider

☐ Water Purifier   ☐ Dropper

☐ Unscented Bleach   ☐ Container For Water

Learn How To Shelter In Place

"Shelter-in-place" means to take immediate shelter wherever you are whether at home, at work or anywhere in between. It may also mean, "seal the room." In other words, take steps to prevent outside air from coming in. This is because local authorities may instruct you to "shelter-in-place" if chemical or radiological contaminants are released into the environment. It is important to listen to TV or radio to understand whether the authorities wish you to merely remain indoors or to take additional steps to protect yourself and your family.

How Do You Prepare?

At home

- Choose a room in advance for your shelter. The best room is one with as few windows and doors as possible. A large room, preferably with a water supply, is desirable, something like a master bedroom that is connected to a bathroom.

- Shut and lock all windows (this provides a tighter seal) and close all exterior doors.

- Have precut plastic sheets to cover all doors, windows and vents in your chosen room.

- Have duct tape to seal off the plastic.

- Develop your own family emergency plan so that every family member knows what to do. Practice!

- Bring your 72 hour kit that includes emergency water and food supplies into the chosen room.

- Seal all openings as shown below.

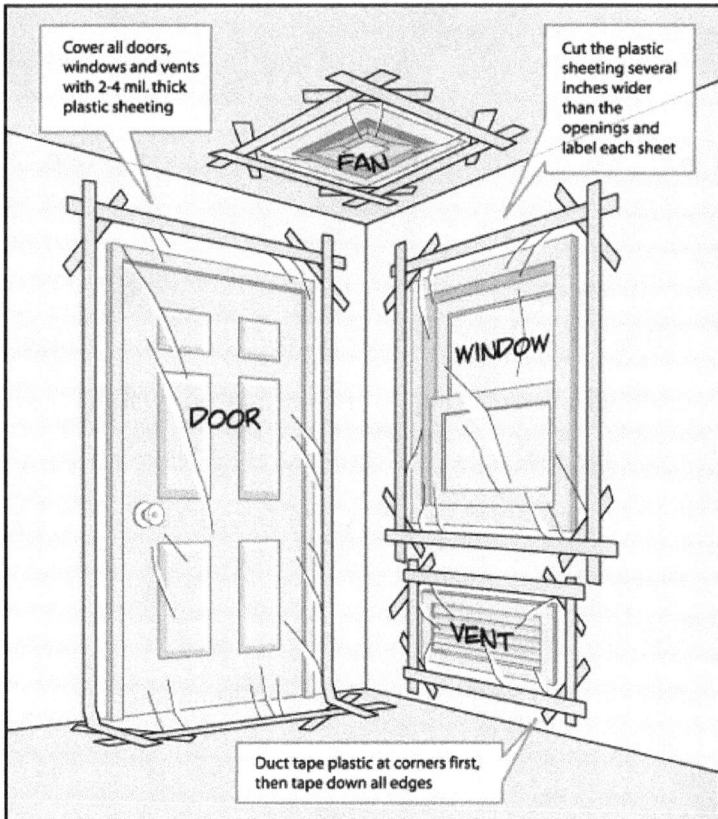

At work

- Help ensure that the emergency plan and checklist involves all employees. Volunteers or recruits should be assigned specific duties during an emergency. Alternates should be assigned to each duty.

- The shelter kit should be assembled. Duct tape, plastic sheets and first aid supplies. A battery operated radio and at least one flashlight with spare batteries should be in this kit. Periodically it is a good idea to refresh the kit and replaceable batteries.

How will I know when I need to "shelter-in-place"?

Fire or police department warning procedures could include:

- "All-Call" telephoning - an automated system for sending recorded messages, sometimes called "reverse 9-1-1".

- Emergency Alert System (EAS) broadcasts on the radio or television.

- Outdoor warning sirens or horns.

- News media sources - radio, television and cable.

- NOAA Weather Radio alerts.

- Residential route alerting - messages announced to neighborhoods from vehicles equipped with public address systems.

I recommend that you do something like I have done. I have chosen the master bathroom as our room to shelter-in-place. It has one door, one window and an exhaust fan. I have in a plastic container one roll of duct tape and plastic cut to size to cover my door, window and vent. I also have some extra plastic and a utility knife. Heavier plastic is best because if you need to open and then reseal the sealed door again the very thin plastic might tear and not be reusable. It is a good idea to have some extra plastic in your kit, in case of rips. Also the kit will then be ready for continued use.

For practice it would be a good idea to use painter's masking tape to seal off the plastic in the practice. Duct tape will likely damage the painted surfaces.

When you are told to shelter-in-place it will typically be for a short period of time. You should also have a battery-operated radio in your kit so that you can know when the danger has passed. A flashlight and food and water from your 72 hour kit will add to your comfort.

Check List Of Items To Consider

- ☐ Plastic cut to fit all openings
- ☐ Duct Tape
- ☐ Utility Knife
- ☐ Battery Operated Radio
- ☐ Water And Snacks
- ☐ Watch Video On Shelter In Place
- ☐ Masking Tape
- ☐ Container for SIP Items
- ☐ Flashlight
- ☐ Extra Batteries For Radio and Flashlight

www.sirvivalpreparednesstips.com has links to a video on shelter in place strategies.

A Simple Roll Of Plastic

The storm takes out several of your windows and the cold night air is filling the house. The rain is falling and entering through the broken windows and falling onto the carpet. You are freezing and you are getting wet. What do you do?

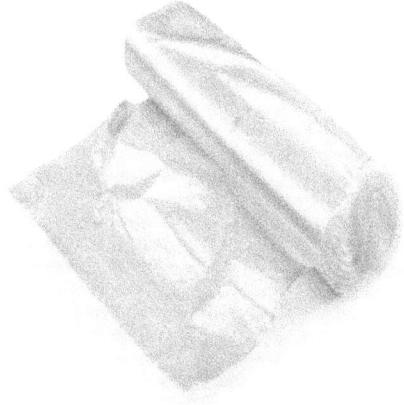

A simple roll of plastic and duct tape will save the day. Every emergency preparedness program should have at least one roll of plastic sheeting. You can buy a roll for $25 at Lowes. This roll is 6mil, very heavy duty and with 250 square feet, it will go a long way.

It would also be a good idea to have a utility knife for trimming the sheeting to the size you need. The sheeting is waterproof, of course, and can also be used as a trap, drop cloth or a covering.

Duct tape is the modern day bailing wire and is universally used to fix things. You should have several full roles stored away in your emergency preparedness storeroom.

Check List Of Items To Consider

☐ Roll Of Heavy Plastic

☐ Duct Tape

☐ Utility Knife

Disaster

Preparedness

Information

How To Survive An Earthquake

It's impossible for any structure to be considered "earthquake proof." Earthquakes vary in type, location and magnitude. Even so, you can take measures to secure a structure before an earthquake and to help minimize potentially dangerous complications afterwards. Knowledge and preparation take away the fear. You cannot eliminate the eventual disaster, but you can minimize its effects on you by knowledge and preparation.

Earthquakes can happen almost anywhere however there are some regions that are at greater risk than others. If you live in one of these areas you should read and ponder these pages. Don't stop with this information. Always be learning and studying. Like a good Boy Scout, "Be Prepared!"

Observe each event as earthquakes occur around the world. Learn from victim's challenges and successes. Continually make adjustments to your emergency preparedness plan as you gain more insights and practical knowledge.

Prepare Yourself And Your Family Now

- Have a 72 hour kit on hand. Plus cash in small bills.

- Plan family emergency procedures, and make plans for reuniting your family afterwards.

- Know emergency telephone numbers such as Sherriff, Police, Hospital Doctor, 911, etc.

- Anchor large heavy objects to the wall such as bookcases, mirrors, other cabinets, water heater, appliances, etc.

- Never place heavy objects over beds or places where people usually sit. A good rule is to keep heavy objects below the head height of the shortest member in the family.

- Educate your family about earthquake safety. Learn what actions you should take when an earthquake occurs. (See next section.)

- Maintain adequate emergency supplies and tools: Battery operated radio; flashlight; first aid kit; bottled water; two weeks of food and medical supplies; blankets, cooking fuel.

- Organize your home for earthquake safety. Store heavy objects on lower shelves. Put your bottled goods on bottom shelves in base cabinets or as low as possible in your pantry. Store breakable objects in cabinets with doors that latch.

- Be sure that any flammable liquids are stored away from potential ignition sources such as water heaters, stoves and furnaces.
- Learn where the main turn-offs are for your water, gas and electricity. Know how to turn them off and the location of needed tools. (See section in this book.)

During An Earthquake Stay Calm And Alert

- **If you are indoors,** stay inside. Move to a safe location such as under a strong desk, a strong table, or along an interior wall. Stay away from windows and glass. The goal is to protect yourself from falling objects and be located near the structural strong points of the room. Avoid taking cover near windows, large mirrors, hanging objects, heavy furniture, heavy appliances or fireplaces.

- **If you are cooking**, turn off the stove, remove the pans from the stove and take cover.

- **If you are outdoors**, move to an open area where falling objects are unlikely to strike you. Move away from buildings, power lines and trees.

- **If you are driving**, stop on the side of the road. Stay away from underpasses and overpasses. Stop in a safe area. Stay in your vehicle. Stay away from trees, large signs, and power lines.

Drop, Cover and Hold On!

This is the recommended action in an earthquake. Drop to the ground, get under some cover and hold on so the cover doesn't shake away. The goal is to protect you from falling objects.

After An Earthquake

- Check for injuries and attend to the injuries as needed. Help ensure the comfort and safety of the people around you.

- Check for gas leaks and water leaks. Check for sewage line breaks. Check for downed power lines and shorts. Turn off the appropriate utilities.

- If you smell or hear a gas leak, get everyone outside. Open the doors and windows. Turn off the gas at the meter. Get at least 200 feet away from the leak. Report the leak to the Gas Company and fire department. Do not use any electrical appliances because even a tiny spark could ignite the gas, yes, something even as simple as a light switch!

- If the power is out, turn off breakers or unplug major appliances to prevent possible damage when the power comes back on. If you see sparks, frayed wires, or smell melting insulation, turn off the electricity at the main breaker. Do not step in water!

- Check structures for damage. If you see excessive damage you should leave it and have it inspected by a safety professional.

107

- Check for additional damage after major after shocks.

- Look for and clean up dangerous spills.

- Always wear shoes, tennis shoes or boots.

- Listen to the radio for public safety instructions.

- Use telephones for emergencies only. This also includes cell phones.

How To Survive a Hurricane

Much of the following comes from the FEMA safety guidelines for hurricanes. I have added a few extra ideas that you can incorporate into your planning as your needs may vary. If you are in a hurricane prone area you'll want to read these guidelines and plan ahead. As I watch disasters around the world I see a great lack of preparedness. I cannot emphasize enough that as you read this book you must study your situation and become knowledgeable. Then develop a plan that is designed for your particular needs. And finally implement the plan.

It also is a good idea to share your plans with others. As you do this you will open discussions that will lead to additional ideas. Keeping in mind that the better prepared you are the better chance you have of surviving any disaster. Take time to become familiar with the next few pages so that you will be well prepared in the event of a hurricane. Hurricanes cause heavy rains and storm surges that can cause extensive flood damage. You should also study the section in this book on flooding.

Before a Hurricane

- To begin preparing, you should build an emergency kit and make a family communications plan.

- Learn the elevation level of your property and whether the land is flood-prone. This will help you know how your property will be affected when storm surges or tidal flooding are forecasted.

- Identify levees and dams in your area and determine whether they pose a hazard to you.

- Learn community hurricane evacuation routes and how to find higher ground. Determine where you would go and how you would get there if you needed to evacuate.

- Make plans to secure your property:

- Cover all of your home's windows. Permanent storm shutters offer the best protection for your windows. A second option is to board up windows with 5/8" marine plywood cut to fit

and ready to install. Tape does not prevent windows from breaking.

- Install straps or additional clips to securely fasten your roof to the frame structure. This will reduce roof damage.

- Be sure trees and shrubs around your home are well trimmed so they are more wind resistant.

- Clear loose and clogged rain gutters and downspouts.

- Reinforce your garage doors. If wind enters a garage it can cause dangerous and expensive structural damage.

- Plan to bring in all outdoor furniture, decorations, garbage cans and anything else that is not tied down.

- Determine how and where to secure your boat.

- Install a generator for emergency power.

- If in a high-rise building, be prepared to take shelter on or below the 10th floor.

- Consider building a safe room.

During a Hurricane

If a hurricane is likely in your area, you should:

- Listen to the radio or TV for information.

- Secure your home, close storm shutters and secure outdoor objects or bring them indoors.
- Turn off utilities if instructed to do so. Otherwise, turn the refrigerator thermostat to its coldest setting and keep its doors closed.
- Turn off propane tanks.
- Avoid using the phone, except for serious emergencies.
- Moor your boat if time permits.
- Ensure a supply of water for sanitary purpose such as cleaning and flushing toilets. Fill the bathtub and other larger containers with water.
- Find out how to keep food safe during and after an emergency.

You should evacuate under the following conditions:

- If you are directed by local authorities to do so. Be sure to follow their instructions.
- If you live in a mobile home or temporary structure – such shelters are particularly hazardous during hurricane no matter how well fastened to the ground.
- If you live in a high-rise building – hurricane winds are stronger at higher elevations.

- If you live on the coast, on a floodplain, near a river, or on an island waterway.
- Read more about evacuating yourself and your family. If you are unable to evacuate, go to your wind-safe room.

If you do not have a wind-safe room, follow these guidelines:

- Stay indoors during the hurricane and away from windows and glass doors.
- Close all interior doors. Secure and brace external doors.
- Keep curtains and blinds closed. Do not be fooled if there is a lull. It could be the eye of the storm. Winds will pick up again.
- Take refuge in a small interior room, closet or hallway on the lowest level.
- Lie on the floor under a table or another sturdy object.
- Avoid elevators.

After a Hurricane

- Continue listening to a NOAA Weather Radio or the local news for the latest updates.
- Stay alert for extended rainfall and subsequent flooding even after the hurricane or tropical storm has ended.

- If you have become separated from your family, use your family communications plan or contact the American Red Cross at 1-800-RED-CROSS/1-800-733-2767.
  - The American Red Cross also maintains a database to help you find family. Contact the local American Red Cross chapter where you are staying for information. Do not contact the chapter in the disaster area.
- If you evacuated, return home only when officials say it is safe.
- If you cannot return home and have immediate housing needs, text **SHELTER** + your ZIP code to **43362** (4FEMA) to find the nearest shelter in your area (***shelter 12345***).
- For those who have longer-term housing needs, FEMA offers several types of assistance, including services and grants to help people repair their homes and find replacement housing.
- Drive only if necessary and avoid flooded roads and washed out bridges. Stay off the streets. If you must go out watch for fallen objects, downed electrical wires, and weakened walls, bridges, roads, and sidewalks.
- Keep away from loose or dangling power lines and report them immediately to the power company.

- Walk carefully around the outside your home and check for loose power lines, gas leaks and structural damage before entering.

- Stay out of any building if you smell gas, if floodwaters remain around the building, if your home was damaged by fire and the authorities have not declared it safe.

- Inspect your home for damage. Take pictures of damage, both of the building and its contents, for insurance purposes. If you have any doubts about safety, have your residence inspected by a qualified building inspector or structural engineer before entering.

- Use battery-powered flashlights. Do NOT use candles. (The flashlight should be turned on outside before entering because the battery may produce a spark that could ignite leaking gas.)

- Watch your pets closely and keep them under your direct control. Watch out for wild animals, especially poisonous snakes. Use a stick to poke through debris.

- Avoid drinking or preparing food with tap water until you are sure it's not contaminated.

- Check refrigerated food for spoilage. If in doubt, throw it out.

- Wear protective clothing and be cautious when cleaning up to avoid injury.

- Use the telephone only for emergency calls. This includes cell phones.

Some Other Items To Consider:

- Turn off the utilities.
- Turn off the propane tanks.
- Filled the bathtubs and large containers with water.
- Contact family members and tell them your plans.
- Have your medications organized and ready to take in case of evacuation.
- Keep your vehicle gassed up and ready to evacuate.
- You would be well advised to have a good raincoat as part of your evacuation supplies.
- Make sure your insurance is both the right type and adequate.
- If power flickers off and on, turn off all of the circuit breakers except the ones that you need for emergency lighting.
- Secure all outdoor objects or bring them indoors. Hanging plants, trashcans, toys and lawn furniture can become projectiles during a storm.

- **NEVER** use a generator inside homes, garages, crawlspaces, sheds, or similar areas, even when using fans or opening doors and windows for ventilation. Deadly levels of carbon monoxide can quickly build up in these areas and can linger for hours, even after the generator has shut off.

- Discuss preparedness ideas with friends and neighbors to get additional ideas. Incorporate into your plan the ideas that are a good fit for your preparedness plan.

How To Survive A Flood

One of the most costly and most often occurring natural disasters in the world is flooding. Every year millions of dollars worth of property and many lives are lost because of floods. Most people in the world, one way or another, are going to experience the after effects of a flood at least once in their lifetime and many will experience regular floods mainly because of where they live. Floods happen in many ways and tend to accompany other disasters such as hurricanes, heavy rainstorms, snowpack with heavy spring run-off, etc. It doesn't matter how a flood may be caused they are extremely destructive, very costly, potentially deadly and can cause major health issues.

Heavy rains can change the landscape, cause mudslides, and fill properties with both mud and water. They can disrupt transportation, take lives and destroy crops. Owners of properties located in "flood plains" should take extra precautions and planning to mitigate damages from the sure-to-come floods. Flood insurance is a must. If you live in a flood plain get it!

If you live in a flood plain here are a few suggestions:

1. Basement walls should be sealed with waterproofing compounds.
2. Consider installing check valves in building sewer traps.
3. You may need a sump pump in your house.
4. Build your home in an elevated manner.
5. Confer with contractors and officials for new ideas.
6. Put your furnace, water heater, and electric panel on a higher floor.

The most important thing you can do is to pay attention to the National Weather Service. They will let you know about floods in advance with their warnings and watches. If emergency personnel tell you that you should evacuate to higher ground, do it! A good rule of thumb is: *When it is comes to flooding...move to higher ground!*

Remember that as little as six inches of moving water can knock you off your feet. 24 inches can float most cars. If you are caught in a flood staying put and waiting for rescue is your best option. Seek safety on the roof of a house. Remember that there are other dangers besides just the running water. There could be poisonous snakes in your area. Dangerous objects are likely submerged just below the surface. Other objects are moving quickly in the flowing water not to mention debris piling up below where you cannot see them and could be pulled under.

A flash flood comes with little to no warning. It is often caused by very intense rainfall. They happen quickly and with little local warning. A thunderstorm many miles away will likely be the culprit. Often there are no dark clouds in your immediate location. The storm that generates the flash flood is likely localized many miles up the canyon.

So don't wait. Begin planning now because it will surely mean unnecessary heartache if you don't.

Planning and preparing for a flood

You should also have a plan for protecting your valuables when you know the flood is coming. Often you will know the flood is coming and have ample time to protect your important items. However, you should only execute your plan to protect your valuables if you have enough time and are not given the order to evacuate by emergency personnel.

A must is to have a 72 hour evacuation kit for any emergency particularly if you may have to evacuate. You'll find more detailed instructions in this book. It is also important that you personalize your 72 hour kit for your needs and the types of disasters you are likely to experience. (See the section on 72 Hour Kits.)

Get Informed. Heed the watches and warnings that are issued in your area. Stay tuned to local weather reports, as well as check in with the National Weather Service.

Be aware of what causes flooding so you can recognize the signs and be better prepared:

- Steady rainfall that lasts for an extensive period of time.
- Heavy rainfall.
- Approaching heavy rains, Tsunami or Hurricanes.
- Weakening dams or levies.
- Rising rivers and streams.

Plan Ahead

There are also steps you can take when a flood is imminent:

1. Move all your furniture and valuable items to the highest area of your home, whether the second floor or an attic.
2. Fill sinks and bathtubs with fresh water in case contamination to the water supply occurs during flooding.
3. Move your outdoor belongings inside.
4. Pack valuables in heavy duty bags, seal and secure.
5. Have a full tank of gas.

Be prepared in case you need to evacuate

FEMA Flood Safety Guidelines:

Be Prepared

- Listen to the radio or television for information.
- Be aware that flash flooding can occur. If there is any possibility of a flash flood, move immediately to higher ground. Do not wait for instructions to move.
- Be aware of streams, drainage channels, canyons, and other areas known to flood suddenly. Flash floods can occur in these areas with or without such typical warnings as rain clouds or heavy rain.

Evacuation

- Secure your home. If you have time, bring in outdoor furniture. Move essential items to an upper floor.
- Turn off utilities at the main switches or valves if instructed to do so. Disconnect electrical appliances. Do not touch electrical equipment if you are wet or standing in water.
- Do not walk through moving water. Six inches of moving water can make you fall. If you have to walk in water, walk where the water is not moving. Use a stick to check the firmness of the ground in front of you.

Driving in Floods

- Do not drive into flooded areas. If floodwaters rise around your car, abandon the car and move to higher  ground if you can do so safely. You and the vehicle can be quickly swept away.

- Six inches of water will reach the bottom of most passenger cars causing loss of control and possible stalling.

- A foot of water will float many vehicles.

- Two feet of rushing water can carry away most vehicles including sport utility vehicles (SUV's) and pick-up trucks.

After a Flood

- Listen for news reports to learn whether the community's water supply is safe to drink.

- Avoid floodwaters; water may be contaminated by oil, gasoline, or raw sewage. Water may also be electrically charged from underground or downed power lines.

- Avoid moving water.

- Be aware of areas where floodwaters have receded. Roads may have weakened and could collapse under the weight of a car.

- Stay away from downed power lines, and report them to the power company.

- Return home only when authorities indicate it is safe.

- Stay out of any building if it is surrounded by floodwaters.

- Use extreme caution when entering buildings. There may be hidden damage, particularly in foundations.

- Service damaged septic tanks, cesspools, pits, and leaching systems as soon as possible. Damaged sewage systems are serious health hazards.

- Clean and disinfect everything that got wet. Mud left from floodwater can contain sewage and chemicals.

After Disaster Strategies

After any disaster, well-planned steps should be taken as the recovery process begins. If you count on the government to assist you, you may be waiting a long time. You must be proactive. You must take the initiative. However, it is important to be cautious; there are many dangers that lurk in the aftermath. Keep your eyes open for dangerous situations. Be aware of your environment. Help those who you can and notify the authorities when it is necessary.

The following information, at times, is redundant and a repeat of information aforementioned. However, I have expanded and organized this information under a general heading to give you general consolidated information that can be used in all situations.

Injuries

Check for injuries. Do not attempt to move seriously injured people unless they are in immediate danger of further injury. Get medical assistance immediately. If someone has stopped breathing, begin CPR. Stop any bleeding injury by applying direct pressure to the wound. Clean out all open wounds and cuts with soap and clean water. Apply an antibiotic ointment and dress the wound. Contact a doctor to find out whether more treatment is needed, such as a tetanus shot. If a wound gets red, swells, or drains, seek immediate medical attention. Have any puncture wound evaluated by a physician. If you are trapped, try to attract attention to your location.

General Safety Precautions After Disaster

Here are some safety precautions that could help you avoid injury:

- Continue to monitor your radio or television for emergency information.
- Be careful when entering any structure that has been damaged. Use the buddy system and keep someone on the outside until safety is determined.
- Wear sturdy shoes or boots, long sleeves, and gloves when handling or walking on or near debris.
- Be aware of hazards such as nails, broken glass and unstable objects.
- Do not touch downed power lines or objects in contact with downed lines. Report electrical hazards to the local authorities and the utility company.

- Use battery-powered lanterns, if possible, rather than candles to light homes without electrical power. If you use candles, make sure they are in safe holders away from curtains, paper, wood, or other flammable items. Never leave a candle burning when you are out of the room.

- Never use generators, pressure washers, grills, camp stoves, or other gasoline, propane, natural gas, or charcoal-burning devices inside your home, basement, garage, or camper—or even outside near an open window, door, or vent. Carbon monoxide (CO)--an odorless, colorless gas that can cause sudden illness and death if you breathe it--from these sources can build up in your home, garage, or camper and poison the people and animals inside. Seek prompt medical attention if you suspect CO poisoning and are feeling dizzy, light-headed, or nauseated.

- Hang up displaced telephone receivers that may have been knocked off by the tornado, but stay off the telephone, except to report an emergency.

- Cooperate fully with public safety officials.

- Respond to requests for volunteer assistance by police, fire fighters, emergency management, and relief organizations, but do not go into damaged areas unless assistance has been requested. Your presence could hamper relief efforts, and you could endanger yourself.

Inspect For Damages

- After any disaster be aware of possible structural damage. Inspect the walls, roof and foundation first from the outside to determine if it is save to enter.

- If you suspect any damage to your home, shut off electrical power, natural gas, and propane tanks to avoid fire, electrocution, or explosions.

- If it is dark when you are inspecting your home, use a flashlight rather than a candle or lighter to avoid the risk of fire or explosion in a damaged home.

- If you see frayed wiring or sparks, or if there is an odor of something burning, you should immediately shut off the electrical system at the main circuit breaker.

- If you smell gas or suspect a leak, turn off the main gas valve, open all windows, and leave the house immediately. Notify the gas company, the police or fire departments, and do not turn on the lights, light matches, smoke, or do anything that could cause a spark. Do not return to your house until you are told it is safe to do so.

- Never use a torch unless you are absolutely sure that you are safe from the dangers of fire and explosion.

Safety During Clean Up

- Wear sturdy shoes or boots, long sleeves, and gloves.

- Learn proper safety procedures and operating instructions before operating any gas-powered or electric-powered saws or tools.
- Clean up spilled medicines, drugs, flammable liquids, and other potentially hazardous materials.
- Watch for hazards when traveling both on and off the road.

Children's Needs

After a tornado, children may be afraid the storm will come back again and they will be injured or left alone. Children may even interpret disasters as punishment for

real or imagined misdeeds. Explain that a tornado is a natural event.

Children will be less likely to experience prolonged fear or anxiety if they know what to expect after a tornado. Here are some suggestions:

- Talk about your own experiences with severe storms, or read aloud a book about tornadoes.
- Encourage your child to express feelings of fear. Listen carefully and show understanding.
- Offer reassurance. Tell your child that the situation is not permanent, and provide physical reassurance through time spent together and displays of affection.

- Include your child in cleanup activities. It is comforting to children to watch the household begin to return to normal and to have a job to do.

Your emergency supplies should be adequate for at least 72 hours (three days). A 10-day supply of water, food, and medicine is a saver recommendation. Always prepare as if you will be the last to receive assistance!

See the following section on 72 hour kits for ideas and suggestions for your kits..

.

Make Your Custom

Emergency

72 Hour Kit

Make Your Custom Emergency 72 Hour Kit

I have seen these three-day kits become more available commercially available, They are in Wal-Mart and now recently at my local independent grocery store. You can easily make your own kit customized to your personal situation. Be sure to update your kit with additional items as your needs and situations change. We will use the next few pages to cover suggestions and ideas you should consider. Make a list of what you need personally and then prepare your 72 hour kit. As you choose the items that you want in your kits keep in mind that each person's needs vary and that you have to carry it. You don't require everything. The list is intended to give you ideas to consider.

Now build an emergency kit to take with you in an evacuation. This is often called a "72 hour kit" or a "Go Bag." The basics should include: enough food and water for at least three days; an extra change of clothes; a sleeping bag or space bag. If

you do not have a sleeping bag a blanket or space blanket is better than nothing. If your kit includes canned food, you will also want a manual can opener.

You should also consider the unique circumstances of infants, the elderly, people with disabilities and others who require special attention. Place all the collected items in a large plastic bag, a backpack or anything that can easily be carried. Remember, this is an emergency situation. Designer-hip look is just not that important.

The best part of this planning is that you probably already have most of the items in your home. So once again, start with a plan and then work the plan. Choose from the following lists what you will put in your evacuation kits. Only pick the items that you need! Remember the weight of the kit is important because you will be carrying it.

Keep in mind that a 72 hour kit will quickly be used up. Many emergencies could last much longer. There are people who wait three to five weeks to get services restored in major disasters. With this in mind, it is a good idea to have a minimum 30 days supply of food, medications and clothing. These items should be securely stored in your home. Even if you have government help, after 72 hours there will be holes in what you need and what they have to give.

Essentials

- ☐ Battery-Powered Or Hand Crank Radio And Extra Batteries
- ☐ Large Kitchen Garbage Bags (To Keep Clothing/Blanket Dry)
- ☐ Blanket (Fleece or Wool Works Great)
- ☐ Manual Can Opener
- ☐ Flashlight And Extra Batteries
- ☐ Food - Ready-To-Eat (See Food Section)
- ☐ One Change Of Clothing
  - o Shirt
  - o Underwear
  - o Sox
  - o Sweater
  - o Pants
  - o Shoes
- ☐ Manual Can Opener For Food
- ☐ Matches / Lighter
- ☐ Emergency Cash in Small Bills
- ☐ Change For Phone Calls
- ☐ Sleeping Bag Or Warm Blanket For Each Person.
- ☐ Additional Bedding If You Live In A Cold-Weather Climate.
- ☐ Water- One Gallon Of Water Per Person Per Day For Three Days
- ☐ _____
- ☐ _____
- ☐ _____
- ☐ _____

Food

☐ Peanut Butter (Protein)

☐ Dried Fruit/Fruit Snacks (Drink Extra Water)

☐ Ramen Noodles

☐ Fruit Cocktail

☐ Instant Oatmeal

☐ Raisins, Prunes, Fruit Leather

☐ Hot Cocoa Mix

☐ Canned Fish Or Chicken

☐ Chips (Best In Tube)

☐ Crackers, Saltine Or Graham Crackers

☐ Nuts/Nut Rolls/Pudding (Other High Protein Snacks)

☐ Granola Bars

☐ Soup

☐ Powdered Milk

☐ Sugar Cookies

☐ Candies That Don't Melt

    o Skittles

    o Candy Corns

    o Starbursts

    o Licorice

    o Taffy

    o Hard Candy

- o Red Vines

☐ Sweetened Cereals

☐ Table Salt

☐ _____

☐ _____

☐ _____

☐ _____

☐ _____

Personal

- ☐ A Copy Of Important Documents (Will Or Trust Information Copies)
- ☐ Additional Warm Clothing If You Live In A Cold-Weather Climate
- ☐ Adults:
    - ○ Books
    - ○ Needle Work
    - ○ _____
    - ○ _____
- ☐ Any Special-Needs Items
- ☐ Cell Phone With Chargers, Inverter Or Solar Charger
- ☐ Children:
    - ○ Coloring Book
    - ○ Crayons
    - ○ Books
    - ○ Games
    - ○ Puzzles
    - ○ _____
- ☐ Copy Of Health Insurance And Identification Cards
- ☐ Don't Forget To Make A Go-Bag For Your Pets
- ☐ Extra Keys To Your House And Vehicle
- ☐ Money
- ☐ Extra Eye Glasses
- ☐ Hearing Aid
- ☐ Cane
- ☐ Crutches
- ☐ Family Photographs

☐ Identification For Each Family Member

☐ List Of Allergies To Any Drug (Especially Antibiotics) Or Food

☐ List Of Emergency Contact Phone Numbers

☐ Local Map

☐ Permanent Marker, Paper And Tape

☐ Photos Of Family Members And Pets For Re-Identification Purposes

☐ Rain Gear/Poncho

☐ _____

☐ _____

☐ _____

☐ _____

☐ _____

First Aid

- ☐ Adhesive Or Paper Tape
- ☐ Baking Soda
- ☐ Bandages
- ☐ Disinfectant
- ☐ Dust Mask To Help Filter Contaminated Air And Dust
- ☐ Elastic Bandage
- ☐ Eye Drops
- ☐ First Aid Kit
- ☐ Hand Lotion
- ☐ Lip Balm
- ☐ Roll Of Gauze
- ☐ Scissors
- ☐ Spirits Of Ammonia
- ☐ Splints
- ☐ Sunscreen
- ☐ Chap Stick
- ☐ Cough Drops
- ☐ Triangle Bandage (37"X37"X37")
- ☐ Tweezers
- ☐ _____
- ☐ _____
- ☐ _____
- ☐ _____

Sanitation

- ☐ Bottle Of Hand Sanitizer
- ☐ Comb / Brush
- ☐ Deodorant
- ☐ Feminine Hygiene Supplies
- ☐ Improvised Toilet Seat (For Bucket)
- ☐ Moist Towelettes, Garbage Bags And Plastic Ties For Personal Sanitation
- ☐ Unscented Liquid Household Bleach (Dilute, Nine Parts Water To One Part Bleach As A Disinfectant)
- ☐ Use 16 Drops Of Unscented Bleach Per Gallon Of Water
- ☐ Personal Hygiene Items
- ☐ Shampoo
- ☐ Shaver
- ☐ Soap
- ☐ Toilet Paper
- ☐ Toothbrush And Toothpaste
- ☐ Wash Cloth And Towel
- ☐ _____
- ☐ _____
- ☐ _____

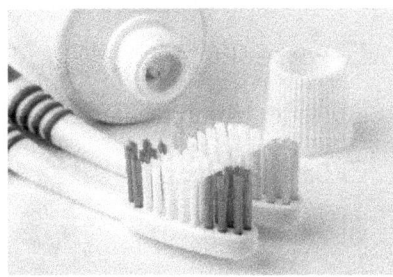

Other

☐ Backpack/Duffle Bag (To Store And Carry All These Items)

☐ Disposable Camera

☐ Heavy String

☐ Fire Extinguisher ABC Type

☐ Work Gloves

☐ Paper And Pencil

☐ Pet Food And Extra Water For Your Pet

☐ Plastic Bags And Ties

☐ Plastic Bucket With Tight Fitting Lid

☐ Plastic Sheeting, Duct Tape And Utility Knife For Covering Broken Windows

☐ Pocket Knife

☐ Reflectors And Flares

☐ Safety Pins

☐ Sewing Kit

☐ Tent

☐ Ground Cloth

☐ Tools:

- ○ Crowbar
- ○ Hammer & Nails
- ○ Staple Gun
- ○ Adjustable

- Wrench
- ○ Bungee Cords
- ○ Rope
- ○ Pliers

- o Saw
- o Screw Driver
- o Shovel

o _____

o _____

o _____

☐ Utility Knife

☐ Whistle To Signal For Help

☐ Wrench Or Pliers To Turn Off Utilities

☐ _____

☐ _____

☐ _____

☐ _____

Special Needs

☐ Individual Medical Needs

☐ Baby Needs

☐ Contact Lens Supplies, Etc.

☐ Infant Formula

☐ Diapers

☐ _____

☐ _____

☐ _____

☐ _____

Cooking Equipment

☐ Mess Kits

☐ Paper Cups

☐ Paper Plates

☐ Paper Towels

☐ Plastic Utensils

☐ Pack Stove

☐ Fuel Bottles

☐ Frying Pan

☐ Cooking Pot

☐ Pancake Turner

☐ Scouring Pad

☐ Dishtowel

☐ Dish Soap

☐ _____

☐ _____

☐ _____

☐ _____

www.ingramcontent.com/pod-product-compliance
Lightning Source LLC
Chambersburg PA
CBHW071131280326
41935CB00010B/1186